NOT WEAKNESS

NAVIGATING THE CULTURE OF CHRONIC PAIN

FRANCESCA GROSSMAN

SHE WRITES PRESS

Published 2023
Printed in the United States of America
Print ISBN: 978-1-64742-477-0
E-ISBN: 978-1-64742-478-7
Library of Congress Control Number: 2022915302

For information, address:
She Writes Press
1569 Solano Ave #546
Berkeley, CA 94707

Cover and interior design by Tabitha Lahr

She Writes Press is a division of SparkPoint Studio, LLC.

A version of the preface was published by The Manifest-Station on October 24, 2019: www.themanifeststation.net/2019/10/24/the-shame-of-pain/.

To Nick, who, against all odds, stayed.
And to Theo and Brieza, who, against all odds, arrived.

"The cure for pain is in the pain."

—Rumi

CONTENTS

PREFACE

I have tried forty-six different times to launch myself out of chronic pain. Every time I try something, I write down what I have done, what it feels like, what it costs, whether it's covered by insurance, and whether it's worth it, in a small purple book. No one knows I do this. I scribble in it like I'm confessing to my sixth-grade diary. It is the same kind of anxiety about the future that I had in sixth grade, just not about Andy Apstein and whether he was going to kiss me or ignore me. Instead, it is about the treatment or therapy I try, and whether this one will be the one to finally help.

The book is twenty-six years old . . . the same age as my chronic pain, more than half my lifetime, and all of my adulthood. Eons.

This book exists because I've had a continuous faith there is a valve for this pain; I can escape it, or more accurately, it can escape me. For all these years, I have *known* this to be true. I will find it. I will heal. I am a warrior, a survivor . . . tough, strong, and able.

People have often told me, "Pain is weakness leaving the body."

I don't have this recorded as studiously as the treatments in my purple book, but I wish I did. I have other lists I don't love revisiting but they help to explain the pain.

Since my diagnosis with Crohn's disease, an illness of the intestines that leads to violent pain and an urgent need to empty my bowels, I have developed ulcerative colitis, a more general type of the disease, which bloats my stomach to appear four months pregnant. I have had surgeries for my stomach, some of which have been determined later to be unnecessary.

I had thyroid cancer throughout my twenties, finally treated when the tumor on my neck was the size of a ping-pong ball. I developed arthritis along the way, both as a peripheral malady and also its own disease.

My body is gouged from piles of polyps removed from my insides, and (usually) benign tumors removed from my outsides. My neck doesn't turn all the way to the right. My hips need forty-five minutes before letting me walk in the morning. I have an unidentified liver problem, which swells without notice and bends me in two. If the saying is to be believed, there's a lot of weakness in there, and it seems to be stuck.

When I was twenty-nine, I had surgery to remove my thyroid. The overnight nurse was a doozy of a lady. Opera-singer large, big, calloused hands that vice-gripped onto my shoulders. Thighs thick as tree trunks, which she used to pin me against the side of the bed so she could administer my IV without "so much squirming." She was brutal and brutish. A small silver peace sign sunk deep into her cleavage, drowning in flesh. She had a hard time getting it in, and as she struggled, she noticed my twisted face.

"Pain is weakness leaving the body, my love," she said, repeating it over and over like a command.

At least once a year, often as much as once a month, this

phrase earworms into my psyche. Whether relating to illness or chronic pain or not, this saying has appeared like a subtitle repeatedly at the bottom of the screen of my life. When I was a weak child? A coach. A teenager who could not stomach even occasional beers? A boyfriend. A young woman unable to go to a bar without scoping out the bathroom situation ahead of time? A roommate. A thyroid cancer patient? A nurse. I have heard it from doctors, PAs, med techs. Physical therapists, friends, masseuses, acupuncturists, pharmacists, bosses, guy on the street.

———————

I went to the doctor a few weeks ago for a routine checkup and a delicate med tech took my vitals. She asked the normal questions, made the normal small talk, took the normal introductory tests. Her thin fingers flew across the keyboard, recording my responses. She asked me if I had any pain.

I wasn't sure I heard her correctly.

"You mean right now?"

"Yes," she smiled softly.

"Nothing acute," I said.

"So no pain?"

"No. I mean, yes, I have pain, the same pain I have all the time."

"What would you rate it on a scale of one to ten?"

How do you rate pain on a scale made for people with no pain?

"I don't know. Four?"

She nodded and her hands took off on the keyboard. It was the wrong answer. I knew this . . . anything under five wasn't worth her noting. Saying four was like saying I had a dull headache or a splinter in my toe. But what should I have said? Seven? Wouldn't that be an alarmist, especially when the pain had been a relative constant for over twenty years? Especially when I knew from decades of experience the litany of potential remedies for the pain was not going to help?

———•———

My husband stepped on a quarter-inch wire sticking out of the ground near the beach in Fire Island one summer. The metal went a good inch into his flesh, and when he pulled it out blood sprayed mercilessly over the sand and sidewalk. He howled. He made noises I'd never heard him make before, and I have been with him through a lot of painful things. He was pale and sweaty, teeth gritting and eyes rolling back . . . that kind of pain.

Later that night, his throbbing foot gauzed and iced, he said, "I'm so sorry you are in pain all the time."

I didn't know how to respond. This wasn't about me. He was the one in pain, and yet a part of me felt smug at his discomfort. *Now you know how I feel,* was a momentary thought I was not proud of. But it got me thinking about pain and the way people relate to it.

It is very hard to relate to pain if you aren't in pain, which is why I have such a hard time with the 1–10 scale.

Instead, for chronic pain patients, med techs and nurses should ask what kind of sharp thing is in your foot. Splinter? Pushpin? Nail? Quarter-inch wire? Razor blade? Glass shard? Burning glass shard?

Nail, I would have said. *Occasionally glass shard.*

But instead, I said four, and she smiled.

———•———

I have fought against my pain and weakness for a very long time. I have tried, often unsuccessfully, to be like my friends. In my twenties, I tried to stay out all night, ski, and walk down the street without doubling over. I worked, I played, I drank, and I sat as still as I could so no one would notice the aftershocks.

In my thirties, I had children. My pregnancies paused my pain for a while, but when it came back it crashed like a tsunami. As is true for many mothers of babies, I didn't sleep and then I had severe postpartum depression. I found having small children so physically demanding I came undone.

Now I'm forty-four, and I am often a prisoner in my house. My stomach bleeds, my liver pulsates, and my head spins. Though not all the time, it happens enough.

From my teens until today, this minute, and all those in the foreseeable future, there is pain. At least nail-in-foot pain, sometimes glass shard. Never pushpin. A splinter would be welcome. When I reflect on my childhood and think of what was difficult—most sports, endurance, gym class, partying, and anything else that required my body to function—it's possible I've been in pain all my life. I have never considered my resting state abnormal, but now I know better. Most people do not live with nails in their feet.

I hurt. I hurt in the morning when I turn over to get up; I hurt when I carry groceries; I hurt when I turn my head to the right to back out my car out in reverse. My stomach burns, my joints swell, and my liver rejects everything I eat and drink.

I don't talk about pain very often. I tell myself it is because people don't want to hear me complain, but it is more than that. I'm ashamed of my pain. I'm ashamed of my weakness.

What is it about pain that is so shameful?

We live in a culture in which wellness equals strength. People my age do CrossFit and triathlons, women have babies without drugs and are lauded for their tight abs, thick skin, and ability to play tough. I have never been strong like that. I have tried but I have failed. I was never scrappy. I don't think I will ever be. I am soft. My belly, the place of much of my pain, is squishy, distended, bloated, or doughy, depending on the day. I'm sensitive. I cry at pop songs.

Our society's greatest hero story is about overcoming obstacles. We love a fighter. We love an underdog who comes out on top. We love triumph and happily-ever-after endings. We love to fix a hoarder, intervene and send someone to rehab, or remodel a decrepit house. We love treatment. We love survival. We love hope.

But hope is complicated. After forty-six different treatments and therapies, I no longer have hope things will get better. I have hope things will not get worse. I have a hope that feels a lot more like mercy than it does like faith.

When I ask myself this question about weakness and shame, I hear a quiet hum suggesting a better question: *Why am I fighting so hard?*

In my experience, pain is not weakness leaving the body. I realize this is a saying, and any mantra is nothing more than a slogan. But slogans have power. They convince. And I'll admit I have always believed this—the suffering I endure might one day let me free.

When I was pregnant and exhausted, a friend of mine told me I was tired because I was making a person. Though not the same, pain sometimes feels like that, too. Of course, I'm tired, I'm fighting against myself all the time, trying to quell the pain so that I can live my otherwise fortunate life.

I'm not delusional about this. I know I live a charmed life in almost every way. I am educated and come from a family that loves me—even when I behave idiotically. I am not from a country ravaged by war. I have a husband who cares for me, does not abuse me, and even dotes on me sometimes. I have two healthy children whom I adore. I am from a privileged minority—I have more than I deserve. I can walk, breathe, and think to exist in my daily life. I can afford therapy, eastern medicine, treatment outside of insurance sometimes, and do part-time work. I can try forty-six things. I'm lucky. Unfairly so. And yet . . .

Everything helps a little. Nothing helps enough to be worth the life-altering work and piles of money it takes to keep it up.

Here's a truth: The things that actually take the pain away feel a lot like the beginnings of addiction. They don't remove the pain. They numb. And they are delicious. But they don't last, and they unleash other pain, often more severe than the original. It's never worth doubling the pain tomorrow to have numbness today, no matter how attractive the reprieve.

So the pain is there. It's always there and most likely it will always be there. I don't know how it got in. Maybe the pain was waiting for me when I came into this world. Maybe it came from my ancestors, my DNA, my parents' tragedies, my childhood bullies, or little or big assaults.

Maybe I am sensitive to the world for some reason, and it simply hurts to be here. As "woo-wooey" as it might sound, it feels the most accurate, the most likely.

I think it's actually softness that makes us strong. It's not skin made of iron. It's showing the underbelly. It's not bracing for the storm, it's putting a kite up in the wind. It's the willingness to see the world as a series of experiences, some of which are going to hurt like crazy, and the ability to just keep going anyway. It's vulnerability. It's asking for forgiveness, from ourselves as much as from others. It's mercy.

Mercy is an open palm. It's the meaty bit. Curling your hand so that your knuckles face the world is so much easier. But a fist to heart feels quite a lot different from a palm to heart, resting square on your breastbone, staying there, the heel of it pulsing the same rhythm as the heartbeat on your chest, marching your body along in an endless trek to some sort of quiet absolution.

My husband's foot healed in a few days. He stopped limping. The knowledge he would get better permeated and defined the experience—the faith it would be over soon.

Therein lies the difference between acute and chronic pain—how we define hope.

What kind of hope can I have? What if I looked at my years and piles of pain and perceived weakness not as a failure but as a step toward becoming who I am? What if I forgave myself the years of fighting myself and sank into the deep, cool water of acceptance?

I do not mean I should give up. I'll try things if they look promising. Add numbers forty-seven, forty-eight, to my book—that's fine. But what if instead of fighting so hard I allow the pain to be part of me? What if, for a while, instead of the restrictive eating and the therapy and the medicine and the exercise and the planning and the trying (and the failing), what if I just stop? Even if it hurts? Even if the pain never leaves? Can I recalibrate to zero? Can I see that as the most radical act? Do nothing at all?

Or, if I cannot stomach complete inaction, what if instead I pivot a little? What if I take the pieces of myself I consider most broken and hold them up to the light?

As I have been thinking about pain and its consequences on my life, I have talked with other people (mostly women) about the pain in theirs. I find, from casual conversations as well as more in-depth research, that many more women are in pain than I ever considered. This is humbling and freeing. Though I should have assumed if I had chronic pain so did a good portion of the population. It has always been easy to feel alone.

As I spoke to women, it became clear to me I was not the only one who felt isolated and singular in my daily life in pain.

Almost everyone felt the same. *What makes us keep quiet?* It couldn't only be the pain that kept us so secluded. There had to be other reasons we felt so disconnected. This book is a quest to find out what those reasons are.

While the pain may always be with us, maybe this feeling of isolation doesn't need to be. Maybe if I can offer a glimpse into my life and the lives of other women who live in pain, it can make us all feel a little less alone. It seems like that's the real work to be done.

So I started to use the little purple book for a new reason. I brought it with me to interviews, scratched down quotes and anecdotes from the women I talked to, scribbled down statistics, and tried to make logical connections.

There are over fifty million people in the United States who live in chronic pain.[1] Of those, almost 70% of them are women.

I am one of those women and I spoke to many more. My aim is to tell an in-depth and honest narrative of what it is like to live a life in pain. I have learned it is different for everyone. The arc of my experience is particular only to me and the arcs of others, uniquely theirs. But despite the differences, I understand some universal truths remain: chronic pain makes life immensely difficult, and it does not go away.

Pain is isolating. The battle is on the inside—constant, relentless, often indescribable, and always exhausting. Pain distances us from those we love, igniting cynicism, depression, and loneliness. Pain doesn't care where you come from, whom you love, where you work, or what you believe in. It just keeps showing up, demanding we pay attention. And when we give pain our attention, we can often feel like no one in the world can understand us—that we are alone in this.

This book is an attempt to show readers in pain they are not alone. It implores them to consider a path of acceptance;

and to respect the reality and truth of their lives even in a world in which they are rarely understood. It is a memoir, and it tells my story with pain, but it is also a chronicle of the culture of chronic pain in our world, and the silence we impart around it. In each chapter, my story will act as the wick, igniting an in-depth exploration of an element of navigating a life in pain.

I'm enormously grateful to all of the women I interviewed, eleven of whom appear specifically in this book. I spoke to twenty-one women about living with chronic pain. While this is clearly a small sample, it proved to me certain themes and issues are prevalent and worth investigating.

What I have found is that there are a lot of us. There are more women in chronic pain in my everyday life than I ever imagined. For me, knowing this has been liberating in a way I didn't expect. I have lived inside the centrifuge of my own pain for so long, I didn't realize I didn't have to be in there all alone. Hearing stories of other women's pain has brought me to a new place in which I can imagine a future of acceptance for all of us.

I can't take anyone's pain away, but maybe in writing my story, sharing others, and rooting them in the complex context in which we live, I can remove some of the loneliness and shame that comes along with it and encourage you to tell your own. I have tried to write my story like an outstretched hand.

This story is my story. But maybe you will see your story here, too. And if you do, my most sincere wish is that my story gives yours voice, makes you feel more connected, and above all else, offers you hope.

BEGINNINGS

The Onset of Chronic Pain

When I was a girl, I had a vivid, recurring dream.

I still remember every detail, every visceral sense. I am bobbing in the ocean. It's warm, which is strange, because it is clearly the Atlantic, the briny water catching my lips, and fuzzy, red seaweed floating by. I am bobbing, fairly effortlessly. The salty water holds me up.

But after a while, I get tired. The current picks up, and the waves flood my mouth and into my lungs. The shore has become a distant sliver of sand. I start to fight for what seems like hours, and my body, face, and lungs become tired, and I decide to give up. This is not a terrifying moment. This is the best moment of the dream. That moment, I let the ocean take me. It's less of a decision and more of a knowing. A safety. A letting go.

I float slowly, without fear or pressure, into the deep. My ears fill up, and my eyes are open but do not sting. I see a blue, silvery fish flutter by. My hair is long and wild in rays around my face. This feeling of giving up and letting myself sink to the bottom of the sea is the best way to describe what I crave so much of the time—to let go.

Almost every time I have this dream, when I reach the moment of blissful acceptance, calm, and security with my inevitable end, I wake up on the shore, curled up inside myself, like a snail, the warm sun beating down on my shell. I feel safe and happy. And just as I accept the engulfing of the sea, I accept this version of an ending, too, my skin tight with salt and seafoam on my toes. I can rest but not drown.

I don't know if this dream was a prelude to my life in pain, but it certainly had its own kind of clairvoyance.

The beginnings of things are sometimes hard to remember, but I have a list of firsts that are quite different from most, and they seem to stick with me.

The first time pain found me was right after the first time I found a lump. I had just downed a can of Arizona Iced Tea. Sweet, soft on the back of my throat, ice cold, and only 99 cents, it was the best deal in drinks. It was August in Massachusetts, and the air was hazy and heavy around my face. I lay face up in my front yard, the prickly summer grass a distant annoyance compared to the throb of my tired muscles. Soccer practice for high school preseason had already begun, burning off the early morning hours with drills I loathed. The Arizona can sweated, and so did my back, in fluid sheets, and I could feel my sports bra forming a damp "O" shape between my shoulder blades. I sat up. I pinched the cotton of my tee shirt between two fingers and pulled it away from my chest, fanning myself with the thin white fabric. Putting both hands inside my shirt, I wriggled out of the sports bra—letting my breasts slap against my chest as I peeled off the spandex.

The tiny marble under my right nipple shouldn't have been noticeable, even to me. But somehow my palm landed directly on it. I rubbed it around for a minute, kneading the circle under my skin, the flesh soft and pliable. I pulled my hand away.

"It's nothing," I decided, lying back down and flipping over onto the yellow lawn, the sharp grass scratching my face, the sun drying my salty neck. The ground felt hard under me, and though I knew it wasn't possible, I felt the little marble roll beneath me, like the princess and the pea. For weeks, I said nothing. My breast turned blue around the nipple, it hurt to touch. Soon my chest bothered me enough that I had to say something.

It took a long time to be diagnosed. At the beginning I was told I had an "undetermined inflammatory disease"— autoimmune in nature. What that meant, practically speaking, was that I would grow small benign growths (not tumors or cysts) that were painful and awkward. Clothes didn't always fit right. The growths were itchy, jutting out from my chest, my hips, my back, my neck.

After a few years, these benign growths became more worrisome nodules and then, in a few cases, tumors. I have since been diagnosed with many more specific autoimmune diseases, including Hashimoto's, thyroid cancer, Crohn's, colitis, and sacroiliac arthritis.

While it is nice to have labels so that insurance companies will pay for some treatments, having all of these diagnoses hasn't really changed anything fundamentally. Regardless of the names, they result in the same thing. I didn't know it then, but that day on the grass was the beginning of my life in pain.

Years later, after surgery to remove my thyroid because of yet another growth (this one malignant), I was in the hospital in the middle of the night without a voice. I really had to pee. I couldn't move my legs and I couldn't talk, my arms were attached to the walls with beeping tubes and clear liquids. I wasn't going anywhere. Eventually, a nurse came into the room, unopened catheter box in hand. She popped the tape with a slit of her bright pink fingernail. I exhaled, thankful.

Quickly, she spilled the pieces of the catheter kit from the pack onto the bed next to my legs, a long tube hitting the floor before she scooped it up. I wrestled with trying to mime to her to not to put the part that had hit the floor in my body, but at this point I was pregnant with pee, unable to think about anything but draining it. She shook out the instructions for the catheter and laid them on the bottom of the bed, smoothing them with her palm. One fingernail held the paper down while another traced the lines of the instructions, one-by-one.

"You've never done this before?" I asked in the loudest whisper I could manage.

"I have. Shh," she replied.

"I'm sorry, but could someone else do it? Someone who doesn't need instructions?" I think I said these words, but I don't think either of us could hear them.

She stopped reading. She looked up at me and let go of the instructions, which fluttered to the floor.

"I've . . . got . . . it," she said slowly.

A half-hour later she had pinned me down, finally inserting my catheter, hanging the tube off the side of the bed, and then lacing it through one of the rails so that it emptied into the pink, putty bedpan she left at the foot. As it filled, she smiled at me, smug and triumphant.

I was so relieved to be draining my bladder I tilted my head back and closed my eyes.

"A 'thank you' would be good," she said.

I ignored her.

When I opened my eyes, she was gone. The urine was still draining from my bladder, overflowing the bedpan bucket, soaking the cotton blanket over my feet. I pressed the nurse's call button. Nothing. I called out, but in nothing more than a hiss. I slept the night with wet legs and a chill that traveled all the way up to the hole in my throat. I couldn't control the tube, so each time my bladder released, my feet went warm for a minute, and then acclimated to the chilly room.

She never came back to change the sheets.

There have been so many firsts like this. My first surgery: benign tumor. My first addiction: benzos. My first MRI: panic attack. My first panic attack: in the MRI. My first financial collapse. My first firing. My first hospital stay. The first friend I lost. The first lie. The first misunderstanding. The first disappointment. The first failure.

And then there have been seconds, thirds, and fourths, and somehow there have not yet been lasts, as far as I can tell.

I don't live in the hole of depression right now. I haven't had surgery in a while. My stomach is calm, at least for today. I can move a little better than I used to. Maybe none of this will ever happen again. This kind of hope is something I am still learning to process.

We have a misguided belief that we control our bodies. We starve them, feed them, and challenge them. We tuck them into jeans. We push them to the very limit, and then we put them to bed, throbbing from effort.

We feel accomplished, empowered, and in control.

But there comes a time when we no longer can support the illusion that we have control. The change can be subtle. It doesn't have to be as life altering as my onset.

For many it's a pimple in the center of your nose, or a cold that knocks you off your feet. Maybe it's a broken finger or a hangover. Maybe it's a a daze. Those are the usual ways. And we should pay more attention because they are the warnings of our youth.

Not that we could heed them. Not that we would.

We don't have control of our bodies. Our wondrous homes function so seamlessly . . . until they don't. One thing can be off—a vein, a cell, a lump—and everything collapses.

We drink water all day and can't quench a thirst. We sleep fifteen hours and wake up as tired as when we put our heads down. We throw up endlessly, assuming we must get it out, but it's not getting out because it isn't something we can get out. It isn't something we can control.

Our brain tries. It tries so hard to stop a pulsing pain, a bleeding gut, or an endless fear. It works and works to will the body into submission.

Of course, there are things we can do to turn the ship a bit. We can sleep well, eat well, exercise, and de-stress. We can have meaningful relationships, we can curb the excess, and we can watch our backs. People say those are tiny things.

To me, they don't feel like tiny things. They feel like boulders. They are so hard to move.

There's no beauty in the pain. Anyone who tells us there is has never been in pain. Pain grabs us by the back of our neck and stares us in the eyes, daring us to close them. But when we close them, when we look away, it comes rushing back, worse because we lost our attention for a minute. We forgot to tense up.

We do not have control.

But . . .

Sitting quietly beside control is belief. Belief is a doughy ally. Belief is a friend. We cannot control our bodies the way we think we can. But we can try to believe that if we are sick or in pain, it is not our fault. We can try to believe in healing. We can try to accept it all even while we hate it all.

Worsening pain and loss of control are so close and always will be. It's all right there in every possible next moment.

Knowing it's there makes me live differently. I wish I could say it makes me appreciate everything more, and sometimes it does, but it also makes me see the world differently. I do not see life as a long path forever unfolding. Instead, life exists to me as a series of moments, some of them exceptionally good, and some of them really bad. They don't necessarily progress. Sometimes they send me back many steps. Thinking like this makes me aware of each moment, knowing the next one could spiral out of control. Because of this I'm careful. I see catastrophe in places it doesn't belong. I hold people at a distance. I stay home more than I should. I worry. I look at the beauty in the world as both a miracle and a warning. *This is so good, it cannot last,* my mind says to me. The truth of beauty is hard to endure. Sometimes it makes me squint at sunsets, just in case.

This book is a compilation of stories of what it's like to live with chronic pain. Though I began by talking to both men and women, it became clear that a lot of women in pain had similar stories, shrouded in a similar culture of silencing, shame, humiliation, and fear. Men had some of those experiences, too, and while I have empathy and respect for everyone in pain, I decided the book would be more focused if I concentrated on women.

Some of the women I spoke to will appear occasionally. Others will be more central in my narrative. Some I spoke to briefly, so while they did not contribute quotes, their experience and thoughts informed the narrative. Some did not want to be identified, so I tell their stories using pseudonyms. Demographics and age were important, and I have listed the breakdown in the appendix.

To make sure there is sufficient context, I share their pain onset stories, in their own words, from those who appear often in the narrative. These women have lived in the shadow of their pain for a long time. My goal is to give them space, voice, and light.

CANDACE

Candace was in a serious car accident when she was in her twenties. Nerve damage and chronic migraines have plagued her for the past twenty-plus years.

Funnily enough, I don't completely remember when my chronic pain(s) started. I do, however, remember the incident leading to the pain.

In the summer of 2001, I was T-boned by a Jeep Grand Cherokee. She drove into my car, which was actually my roommate's car—a big, blue Volvo (which was boxy but good). My roommate asked/allowed me to drive it so it didn't sit unused on campus.

The SUV hit me on the passenger side, which was the best luck I had that day.

I've forgotten the details of many of the things that happened that year. There's the 9/11 attacks, a train trip I took just after the attacks, and the accident, which happened a few weeks, maybe a month before the attacks. I don't remember the date of the accident, but I remember in vivid detail watching the SUV bear down on me and thinking, "She's going to hit me."

And then she did.

I'd heard people often experience moments of crisis in slow motion, which was definitely true for me. Once I realized she was going to hit me, it felt like everything slowed down.

When you hear cars crash in a film, the sound is almost like a chord—a low thud of heavy things colliding, mid-tones of skidding tires and scraping metal, and the high-pitched tinkling of shards of glass.

But I only heard the flat punch of the impact, and then everything went silent. I don't remember the sound of the window breaking, but I remember how it was whole and then suddenly wasn't. She wasn't going to stop until it was too late. But when she hit me, my vision grew sharp enough to see each tiny piece of shattered glass hang suspended, just for an instant before they started to fall. Surprisingly, more of it ended up on the hood of the other vehicle than inside the car. I remember watching the passenger side curve in toward me and wondering if it would keep coming, and I remember screaming, but not because I was afraid of getting injured: my laptop was on the passenger seat, and my dissertation-in-progress was on the laptop.

It's probably telling, and not in a positive way, that at a moment when I should have been afraid for my well-being, if not for my life, the scariest thing to me was my dissertation might get destroyed. Nothing seemed quite real. Then, after what felt like minutes but was probably milliseconds, physics caught up with me. My left thigh came up off the seat a little as my body fell to the right, my right ear meeting my right shoulder. Then I was flung the other way, and my hearing kicked back in just in time to hear three staggered "thumps" as the left side of my body—first the arm near the elbow, then the shoulder, and finally my head—slammed into the driver side door and window.

The accident happened a few yards away from the campus police and fire stations, so help came quickly. I don't remember getting out of the car, but I remember a kind police officer holding a clipboard over my face while I was strapped down, face up, immobilized on a stretcher. It was kind of her, but I thanked her most profusely when she rescued my dissertation before I got separated from the car.

I was in full-on Robocop mode for a few days after the accident—I couldn't turn or lean my head to the left at all and could barely do so to the right. I don't remember how long it took to get over the acute injury. But several months later, after I thought I was fine, I started experiencing a set of symptoms no one (including me) tied to the accident for a long time: debilitating headaches (typical migraine) and a network of other symptoms including neck pain and stiffness; burning nerve pain in my head, neck and arm; numb fingers; and a sensation like something clawing its way out of my right eye like the chest breaker in *Alien* (atypical migraine). Over time, the typical migraines became fairly rare, but the atypical went from occasional to frequent to chronic, and I spent a good (that is to say horrible) portion of the next two decades feeling like someone had poured a trail of gasoline down my right side and set it on fire.

EMILY

Emily has had pain, migraines, fainting spells, and arthritis all of her life. She started to notice pain when she was a child, and things have evolved ever since.

I began having migraines when I was ten years old. I got mono when I was sixteen and the fatigue was crushing, never seeming to abate. After giving birth at twenty, the fatigue got even worse, but now I had a new tiny human to care for, so I doubled down on self-discipline to finish my degree. It took several years to complete my bachelor's, but I did.

At age twenty-nine, I worked two jobs and began experiencing pain in my left knee. I'd always chalked it up to an old sports injury, but then my right knee began hurting, and then my hips. The pain continued to accumulate in all of my large and small joints. I wore knee and elbow braces, back braces, and arthritis gloves. My doctor told me to quit one of my jobs. I did. And then I slowly cut down my hours on my other job until, at the age of thirty, I was unemployed and bedridden by this mysterious pain.

JESSICA

Jessica has scoliosis and has been in intense back pain since her early teens.

I was diagnosed with scoliosis when I was in ninth or tenth grade. I wasn't in any pain, but one day my mom was hugging me and noticed one side of my back stuck out more than the other. My parents took me to an orthopedic doctor, and I was diagnosed with scoliosis. My curve was S-shaped and because the top and bottom curves balanced each other out, I stood up straight and wasn't hunched over or off balance. We were told I wasn't a candidate for surgery because my curvature wasn't severe enough, and I didn't need a brace because I was basically done growing. The curvature likely wouldn't worsen. I remember being given some stretching exercises to do regularly, but that was it.

I don't remember anyone mentioning anything about pain I might experience from age-related spine compression over time. I'm not sure about the specific onset of my pain. I know by my mid-twenties, I was in enough pain I was getting massages and seeing a quirky chiropractor. He had developed his own therapy that worked on breaking up scar tissue and getting people in better alignment. I could write a completely separate story about this guy, but the treatment did give me some temporary relief. (As an aside, the treatment also caused me to be very sore for a couple days after each appointment, so it did cross my mind that the relief I felt may have just been relative to the increased post-appointment pain!) It was through this man that I bought a fur-lined clavicle brace to wear around my apartment. This contraption held me in a stretching position that felt nice and maybe was meant to improve my posture. I wanted to try anything to address the pain.

I knew my pain was probably going to be an issue—as in my scoliosis wasn't going to go away—but I didn't think of myself as a person dealing with chronic pain.

The many years since then have been an up-and-down journey. I've had some periods of acknowledging the pain as part of my life and trying to be proactive in managing it (the chiropractor, the clavicle brace, various rounds of physical therapy, muscular activation, steroid injections, pain medications and so much more. I shudder to think about all the money I've spent on treatments and accoutrements). I pushed through the pain, denied it as an issue, pretended I was fine, and didn't adjust my life at all.

There have been some periods of knowing the pain as part of my life and feeling hopeless, angry, frustrated, overwhelmed, and unmotivated to work on it. A graph of this journey wouldn't be linear.

It's probably only in the last three to five years that I've actually started using the term "chronic pain" in reference to myself. I think I've known that's what it was for a long time, but I hadn't named and acknowledged it. Even though professionals have told me repeatedly that my pain is something that isn't going to resolve and will just need to be managed, I don't remember anyone saying the specific words "chronic pain" to me. Was I waiting for a diagnosis from someone else to validate it? Was I not wanting to admit it to myself because it sounded too depressing, scary, wimpy, or dramatic? Was I brushing it off in order to protect my parents, who still feel guilty when I mention my pain because they wonder if they should have done more sooner? Was I denying my reality to protect myself? Even in deciding to participate in this project, I found myself questioning whether I belong—whether I "counted" as someone who experiences chronic pain.

Today, I know the truth and continually work on accepting it. I know how real and impactful my pain is to me. I know I am reminded each day of my pain countless times—by an ache, a sharp pain, a stiffness, a need to stretch, a range of motion issue, or a flare-up; by sitting, standing, walking, cooking, cleaning, raking, or exercising; by doing almost anything for too long; by automatically thinking how any activity will feel on my back; and by feeling deterred from a lot of activities, which would sound great, if I had a better back.

KATE

Kate was diagnosed at twenty-three with a rare neurological disorder called Trigeminal Neuralgia (TN). TN makes makes the neurons in her face burn at the slightest touch.

I was twenty-three years old. I lived with a family as a live-in nanny while I went to graduate school. It was autumn, October, I think. One night, after the girls were tucked in and the house was quiet, I washed my face before bed. I splashed the water up and on my cheeks and felt a jolt on the left side of my forehead, a sensation difficult to describe. That was the first one. I remember touching my face afterward, poking it and tapping my forehead. And nothing happened. So I went back to washing, splashed water on my cheeks a second time, and it hit me again—a bolt of lightning through my face, hot and electric, hard enough I had to grip the sides of the sink to keep standing. It was then when the fear hit, too.

I figured, like most things, I would be completely fine the next day. But I wasn't. I was walking down the street in Cambridge. It was windy, and the electric pain came back so hard and fast, I stopped on the sidewalk and turned my back to the wind—turned away from the wind and away from the pain. But I couldn't get away from it. I turned and spun in place on the sidewalk. And then I froze. I was afraid to move. I remember thinking I was going to be stuck on that sidewalk forever. But I turned, slowly, and made my way to my boyfriend's, where I climbed into bed. I was in that bed for days. I was in too much pain to do anything. Every time I touched my face, it felt like I was holding a live wire to the top of my head as the current ran down the left side, through my eye, to my front tooth.

KATIE

> Katie suffered from a cecal volvulus, the rotation or torsion of a mobile cecum and ascending colon, which caused her to be hospitalized for over a month.
>
> The condition is very serious, sometimes fatal. She suffers residual issues from two subsequent colon surgeries, generally defined as irritable bowel syndrome/inflammation/scar tissue in the colon.

I was driving to Tahoe with a friend when something happened—a mild stomachache was turning into something more sinister, a kind of pain I'd never felt before. It was like thick, rubbery snakes were wrapping themselves around my intestines, pulling, twisting, and sinking their fangs into my flesh. Sweat started pouring down my forehead. Until then, I hadn't known "blinding pain" was more than an expression—the pain could make the world disappear immediately. By the time I was carried through the sliding glass doors of the ER, I was drenched in my own sweat and drifting in and out of consciousness.

LESLIE

Leslie has lived with inflammation and pain her whole life. She was eventually diagnosed with endometriosis and subsequently suffered two serious car accidents in the span of a couple of weeks. She was later diagnosed with osteoarthritis and Achilles tendonitis.

She also lives with allergies and immune responses so severe, she must carry medicine with her all the time.

I don't remember a time without pain. I spent most of my life with monthly migraines and ear infections, and later was diagnosed with endometriosis. I didn't realize most people don't experience such severe pain regularly until I was in high school. It took years of adjusting to the reality of unknown autoimmune diagnoses, managing the symptoms, and getting no answers. During this time, I was in two major accidents four weeks apart. My car flipped down a 100-foot ravine, and I walked away with spine and head injuries. While rehabbing from the car accident, I was hit during an international bike race and thrown over a five-foot fence. I regained consciousness as I was wheeled into the ER with another concussion, sprained ankle, and more back issues.

Months of rehabilitation and physical therapy helped me function on a daily basis, but there was always underlying pain. I didn't know the difference between good and bad pain, so

I continued to be active and move, which caused additional damage. Because I was compensating for the pain from the injuries, I stopped using my major muscles. Using only my minor muscles altered my gait and body alignment and increased my mobility and arthritis issues. After finding the right doctors and months of tests, MRIs, X-rays, etc. they determined my spine was pinching nerves and I had osteoarthritis and Achilles tendonitis and an inability to flex my feet. With a plan in place, I continued to have weeks where I couldn't walk or put any pressure on my foot. While I was happy to have this addressed, the as-yet undiagnosed autoimmune issues caused more serious problems and multiple ER visits a year. My allergies affected my asthma and caused me to have hives and anaphylaxis. I had endured years of doctors' visits and tests and still no explanation why this was happening.

In 2013, I found an amazing allergy and immunology doctor who ran a new set of tests and determined I had autoimmune urticaria and anaphylaxis. I carried epipens, a slew of meds and prednisone, and a list of steps to take when a reaction starts to avoid the ER. Since a new drug came out to manage asthma and autoimmune urticaria, I have been been under control for the past few years. It's been a lifesaver and for the first time in many years, I have moments of peace.

Most days, I wake up with pain in my hip and back. Lately, my allergies are out of control, and I am constantly itchy and sensitive to touch. Last week, I couldn't put any pressure on my foot for three days. The unknowns are the hardest. I've had days where I am in tears at the end of the night because I can't get up the stairs. It's at those moments I worry what the next forty-five years might be like knowing how much I hurt now.

Prior to COVID, my husband traveled almost all year so I was the primary caregiver for our child.

We have no family in the area, so everything falls on me. No matter how I feel, I still have to get him to school, activities, etc. I have learned to push past the pain and make things happen. There's no other option. Some nights I break down and cry, hoping the next day will be better. I've learned to adjust my expectations of how much I can accomplish depending on how I feel. I am more aware of how to take care of myself and listen to my body.

MICHELLE

Michelle was a child gymnast and suffered a severe back injury tumbling as a late teen. This has resulted in life-long, chronic back pain.

I was nineteen years old and excited to watch my old gymnastic team compete in a meet at my high school. After the meet ended, I was inspired to do a tumbling pass on the wooden gym floor. As my feet left the ground, I knew immediately I was not going to make the back tuck and within that split second, I tucked my head to my chin to brace my fall and to protect my neck. The wind got knocked out of me when I landed on my back, and I was embarrassed and hoped no one saw that I did not complete my back tuck. My best friend saw me on the floor and asked me if I was lying down because I was tired. For the first five seconds (which felt like fifteen minutes), I could not move my legs and thought I landed on my neck and was paralyzed. Then the thought of an ambulance coming in and taking me out on a stretcher made me panic about the fuss and scene I would make. I vaguely remember getting up and getting in my car to drive home. When I got home, someone asked me how the meet was and then put their hand on top of my back. I burst into tears and told one of my parents how much pain I was in. They took me to the emergency room at Newton Wellesley Hospital, where I proceeded to be a brat about them wanting to cut my favorite sweater to get access to my neck.

At first, they could not see anything wrong with my X-rays. However, they called in another doctor for a second opinion when they realized I was having some shortness of breath. After a few hours, it was determined that I had a compressed vertebrae fracture on my T9. It didn't seem like much, but the 8% compression has led to twenty-three years of chronic pain.

It started off as an isolated pain in the general area but has progressed to being pain in my neck and my entire back. The new norm has become living life numb to the pain and getting chiropractor and acupuncture treatments to help manage the days when things don't feel so numb.

RACHEL

Rachel suffered from pain her whole life and was eventually diagnosed with Ehlers-Danlos hypermobility syndrome, a genetic disorder affecting connective tissues and causing an array of serious physical problems, ranging from joint pain to cardiovascular issues.

I always remember having pain as a small child in places like my low back, but it was never anything serious enough that required a doctor. I saw chiropractors as a teenager, and when I was around eighteen or nineteen years old, I started having pain in my shoulders. By my mid-twenties it was pain in my upper back, which was very connected to my menstrual cycle. My whole body was in pain whenever I was about to get my period. After my first child was born, I started having more and more pain on a regular basis, and there was not a lot of explanation for what I was going through.

By the time my youngest was born, I was having even more issues. My thyroid stopped working, and I was in pain almost all the time. I was always tired, and I had to be hospitalized, although they couldn't determine what was wrong with me except I had no potassium at all in my body. It was the most pain I'd ever been in, and it paralyzed me. I couldn't move my legs, and I was having hip spasms worse than labor pain. Later, I was diagnosed with Ehlers-Danlos hypermobility syndrome.

SAMANTHA

Samantha was in a near-fatal riding incident in the mid '90s, which left her with severe, constant, chronic pain in her leg and shoulder.

This started after a horseback riding accident—although, to be fair, I've had many bad accidents in my life, and only now in my fifties realize what a toll all of it took on my body. But the really bad accident—the one that could have killed me—happened out in a canyon. I'd taken my horse for a ride on a trail I'd never been down before. It's a long story—I wrote a book about it!—but my horse trampled me in a freak accident, dislocating my shoulder and severing much of my lower left leg. I was lucky to be rescued before I bled out. Doctors were able to put my leg back together, although my surgeon warned me it would probably be better if they amputated. After about a year, it really sunk in that the pain I felt in my leg, and the stiffness and ache in my shoulder, were going to be my companions for the rest of my days.

Three of the women I feature in this book preferred not to be identified. Therefore, I will use pseudonyms for them and will do my best to remove any identifying pieces of information. To give a sense of their onsets, here are their brief pain backstories:

Adele has had rheumatoid arthritis for over thirty years. RA is an autoimmune and inflammatory disease, which means the immune system attacks healthy cells in the body by mistake, causing inflammation (painful swelling) in the affected parts of the body. RA mainly attacks the joints, usually many joints at once.

Dolores has fibromyalgia—a condition causing pain all over the body (also referred to as widespread pain), sleep problems, fatigue, and often emotional and mental distress. She has been in pain for over forty years but was only diagnosed and treated fourteen years ago.

Sheree was in a car accident that left her spine twisted. When she sits down, she leans almost forty-five degrees to the right. She is in constant back pain, which intensifies when she sits or carries her small children.

SILENCING

When Suffering Is
Dismissed and Ignored

The first time I had serious surgery (more than an outpatient procedure to remove a lump), I had my thyroid removed. If there is a better metaphor for being silenced than to have your throat cut out, I don't know what it is.

I had spent eight years telling doctors something was wrong with me. It had been about fifteen years since I knew something was off. Each time I went to the endocrinologist for my thyroid, I would choke back tears when he told me everything was fine.

I hadn't switched doctors in eight years, and he still hadn't learned how to say my name. In retrospect, I should have been strong enough to correct him, or to leave, or to find another doctor in a city teeming with them. But I barely had enough energy to chew my food, which indicated how monumental it would have felt to change doctors. This guy was a "Best of New York." This guy was someone I had been referred to by my friend, a med student. This guy had forty years of work under his belt. I only had fifteen of pain under mine. So I kept going back, first once a year, then once a season, then once a month, to check on the lump in my throat, which first the size of an almond, then a walnut, and finally, when I was twenty-nine years old, zeroing in on ping-pong ball territory.

"So listen, Frances-sa. I know we said it all looks fine, and it does—*it does*. All the biopsies we always do have come back clean, and your thyroid level is well within the accepted range. . . ."

I had my thyroid level checked seemingly hundreds of times in that eight-year period. Every kind of doctor I went to, from my gastroenterologist to my PCP to my therapist, all ordered thyroid tests. They always came back "normal."

A normal thyroid hormone range is 0.5 to 5.0 mIU/L.

Sometimes I was at 1.5, sometimes 4.5, but never too high or too low to be worrisome to doctors.

This, I have since learned, is common for people with thyroid disease. Thyroid levels can change day by day, time of the month, or time of the year. The only way to really know if your thyroid is functioning properly is to take blood often and see how much it fluctuates.

According to doctors, my thyroid was fine. I had already been diagnosed with Crohn's disease and some other inflammatory issues, so doctors attributed my fatigue and pain to those issues, dismissing my assertion there was something terribly off with my thyroid. It was doubling in size.

"So lean back, and I'll take the biopsy and, well—wow, that nodule has gotten sizable."

"Yes, I thought so too," I started to speak, but a long, thick needle was aimed at my throat and the same doctor, hovering above me, said:

"Shhhhh."

The next few days were a whirlwind. The biopsy was malignant (in previous biopsies he had found only benign tissue), and surgery was scheduled. I had cancer and then in two days, I didn't. But I had had it for eight years. Eight years of no one believing me when I said things were wrong. The nodule had grown too fast, it hurt to swallow and I had difficulty speaking. And then in an instant it was gone. My throat was cut.

I know it was not as simple as that, but I felt silenced in an extreme and brutal way—first by being ignored and then by treating me. And the worst part was I was right.

As I have been talking to women about their pain, there is no more common response than an anecdote about feeling silenced. Whether it is by their families, or partner, their friends or, most often, the medical professionals they see, women in pain feel as though they are not heard, or worse, they are embarrassed into silence.

Kate, who at twenty-three was diagnosed with a rare neurological disorder called trigeminal neuralgia (TN), recounted the following story, which stuck with her:

"There is one minute, one sentence, which I think about— all . . . the . . . time . . . even fifteen years later because of its impact.

"After *finally* getting a TN diagnosis and living with pain for a couple of years, I made an appointment to see an ENT specialist because I had chronic sinus infections. Those infections, as you can imagine, made the TN pain worse. I'd have a full sinus infection and constant nerve attacks because of it. Talking, breathing, and blowing my nose were all triggers when I had an infection.

"At the appointment, a medical fellow entered the room first. She was slight, with dark, short, curly hair. Female physicians always made me feel more comfortable, so I was glad to see her. She introduced herself as my doctor's fellow and asked me why I was there. As always, when at appointments, I started to give a preface about my TN.

"'I have trigeminal neuralgia on the left side of my face. It started in branch 1 but has grown to include branch 2. My pain is compounded by sinusitis, to the point where I will feel pain in the third branch as well—'

"She put her hand up to stop me. 'I'm sorry,' she said, 'are you a physician?'

"'No,' I answered.

"She put her hand down and shook her head. 'OK.' She smiled. 'Then just show me where it hurts.'

"I froze for a second, shut my open mouth, and silently pointed to the left side of my face. I did not speak another word to her. I was so shocked, angry, and humiliated that I even argued myself out of reporting her to the doctor when he came in. I don't know what prompted her to say that to me—my correct use of language about my own rare condition. Maybe she thought I was "too young" to have TN. Maybe it was her own insecurity in her own position as a student. Maybe she believed that a patient couldn't possibly know more than someone who went to medical school. I don't know. What I do know is that the memory of that woman's words silencing me still makes me shake with anger."

What Kate experienced is prevalent. In the 2001 study, *The Girl Who Cried Pain: A Bias against Women in the Treatment of Pain*, the authors explain "women are more likely than men to be undertreated or inappropriately diagnosed and treated for their pain."[1] Maybe this is simply a general bias against women, but I have a feeling it is something else.

In this study, along with many others with similar out-comes, researchers found women are more likely to be offered sedatives than pain medication by medical professionals when they describe their pain. Calming them down, not treating their pain, is the operative. Why does this difference exist? The study found many health-care professionals feel "women are not accurate reporters of their pain; men are more stoic so that when they do complain of pain, 'it's real.'"[2]

As *The Girl Who Cried Pain* study concludes, "Men are taken more seriously than women when it comes to reporting pain. But it's not only that, women are dismissed, condescended to, and ignored, often leading to them avoiding to address pain in future situations and keeping them home, suffering, and often perpetuating diseases and injuries that can lead to more and more difficulties down the line, sometimes fatal ones."[3]

As I talk to women, it becomes clear this trend of keep-ing quiet is something many of them have experienced, often repeatedly. All of the studies I have read indicate the data is con-sistent, but there is something else needling me. It's not only the medical profession that is silencing women, it's the media too, and the culture in which we live. We repeat the patterns we learn; we pay attention to where our attention is called. There is an overwhelming cultural impression that suffering in silence somehow makes us stronger, or that being quiet about our pain should be lauded. This is baked into our understand-ing of our world from the second someone calls us brave when we don't cry in kindergarten, or praises us for "manning up" on the soccer field, or congratulates us for getting over our grief quickly and without too much drama. We are conditioned to feel like silence *is* strength, and I think that's a real problem.

While she hasn't felt silenced by the health-care profes-sionals she has seen, Michelle, who's acute back injury from a gymnastics accident left her with lifelong chronic pain, takes this cultural norm to heart.

> "You always hear people say, 'suffer in silence' or as a former athlete, 'suck it up,' and 'no pain no gain.' I was never really quieted or ignored by doctors when I talked about my pain, (which I rarely do because of the 'I should really suffer in silence' mentality), but I felt people judged me and thought I was overreacting or dramatizing the extent of my pain (again better to suffer in silence).
>
> "The pain I have isn't a pain seen with the naked eye. I don't have a gash on my back, and I don't wear a brace. I am not hunched over from a compressed vertebra. When something physical is not seen, it's harder to understand the true nature of my pain. Someone, however, can equate and relate to, 'Oh yes! Ouch that might hurt.'
>
> "I see the skepticism in people's eyes when I tell them why I am being an angry, irritable bitch. I tell them sometimes the constant, everyday pain makes it feel like I have a ton of bricks resting on my upper back. I tell them the weight I feel on my shoulders is so heavy, I just want a break from the heaviness. I tell them I am tired, and it's tiring to constantly feel like you are carrying bricks every day.
>
> "It doesn't feel like I'm being *ignored* when I speak of my pain, it's more like people dismiss the extent of my pain because they can't physically see 'hurt' on me."

While we cannot assume all dismissal and mistreatment result in silencing, we have to acknowledge there is an inherent gender bias in our health-care system, which can be extremely dangerous. A 2000 study published in *The New England Journal of Medicine* found, "Women are seven times more likely than men to be misdiagnosed and discharged in the middle of having a heart attack. Why? Because the medical concepts of most diseases are based on understandings of male physiology, and women have altogether different symptoms than men when having a heart attack. To return to the issue of chronic pain, 60% of the people it impacts are women. And yet, 80% of pain studies are conducted on male mice or human men."[4]

It isn't surprising when women speak up about their chronic pain, they are often ignored. This reality permeates the medical system at large but is particularly evident in emergency situations in which pain must be assessed quickly so that patients can be seen and treated in order of severity.

In his Atlantic piece, *How Doctors Take Women's Pain Less Seriously*, Joe Fassler explains how this kind of bias, sexism, and silencing played a serious role in his wife's emergency treatment.

Presenting with severe abdominal pain, she was passed over multiple times over fourteen-and-a-half hours before she was diagnosed with "ovarian torsion, a horrific, blindingly painful condition that led her to emergency surgery."[5] He was outraged at this treatment.

When I read Fassler's account, I did a double take. I was shocked that he thought fourteen-and-a-half hours was a long time to wait for treatment, even when one was in excruciating pain. To me that amount of time sounded normal.

I have, and I know many other women who have, in their unrelenting pain, waited like wallflowers on the periphery of ERs, clinging to gurneys and clutching johnnies closed, praying someone will give them a minute of attention. All of us have spent hours waiting at clinics and doctor's offices, only to be passed over for men who are louder, taken more seriously, and rarely in more immediate need. Though I have infrequently been in the kind of excruciating, acute pain Fassler describes his wife having, I have sometimes waited more than fourteen-and-a-half *months* to be heard.

"Emergency-room patients are supposed to be immediately assessed and treated according to the urgency of their condition. Most hospitals use the Emergency Severity Index, a five-level system that categorizes patients on a scale from 'resuscitate' (treat immediately) to 'nonurgent' (treat within two to 24 hours)."[6]

But that is not the case in many emergency rooms and other urgent care scenarios, certainly not ones I have been in.

Again, I was baffled by Fassler's surprise. I didn't understand why he was shocked that his wife was being dismissed. Why did he think things would happen quicker? And then it hit me. His wife got treated in only fourteen-and-a-half hours because *he* was with her, and *he* was advocating for her. If she had been alone, she might not have been heard at all or seen at all; she may have been shushed, silenced and dismissed, leading, possibly, to her death.

When I asked Emily, who struggled with debilitating joint pain, connective tissue disease, autonomic dysfunction, and migraines since she was twenty, if she had experience with this kind of silencing, she said the following:

"When I began experiencing joint pain at twenty-nine, the rheumatologist I saw dismissed me when I told him an anti-inflammatory was barely touching the pain. I then saw a slew of specialists over the next several years, the majority of whom told me or alluded to the idea, 'it was all in my head.' I was dosed with an array of psychotropic medications, which numbed me out emotionally where I couldn't function mentally, while still experiencing intense physical pain. This went on for years.

"It would be ten years before a correct diagnosis of two different connective tissue diseases and autonomic dysfunction (which caused scary fainting spells, since at that time I lived by myself) was made. When I was finally heard, believed, and treated/medicated properly, it was as if a 1,000-pound boulder had been lifted."

Emily is not alone. According to the New York Times piece, *Women Are Calling Out 'Medical Gaslighting,'* "Women say doctors frequently blame their health problems on their mental health, weight, or a lack of self-care, which can delay effective treatment . . . research suggests that women are twice as likely as men to be diagnosed with a mental illness when their symptoms are consistent with heart disease."[7]

In *The Girl Who Cried Pain*, the authors state women are "more likely to be treated less aggressively in their initial encounters with the health-care system until they prove that they are as sick as male patients, a phenomenon referred to in the medical community as 'Yentl syndrome.'"[8] It is accepted as practice to disbelieve. It is as if they listen more to women, they might be wasting their time.

Rachel, who suffers from Ehlers-Danlos hypermobility syndrome, an incurable connective tissue disorder, agreed that silencing was a huge factor in how long it took her to be diagnosed.

She told me,

"I have had many experiences with silencing. It is not uncommon for many individuals who have EDS to be written off as just pill-seekers or hypochondriacs. This is for a variety of reasons, but mostly because it affects the entire body, so it is hard to be taken seriously by anyone."

She recounted the following specific experience:

"I walked into the office of an orthopedic surgeon in State College in Pennsylvania where I was living at the time. The doctor was very dismissive and refused to do any MRIs. He asked me multiple times why was I there because, I 'looked fine.' He then told me to save my money and fly back to Atlanta if I needed anything done because they wouldn't be able to do it.

"The doctor then looked at me and said, 'You know, I have another patient. She's almost half your age and she is in way worse condition than you. She looks like she's in way more pain than you.'

"What he really was saying was that I had makeup on and that I was able to function, and so he just wrote me off because I didn't look sick enough. He wouldn't hear me because he had made the decision by looking before he ever listened."

I wonder about all of the silence we, as women in pain, are shrouded in. We are conditioned to be quiet, both because of our experiences but also our culture. It is part of my reason for writing this book. We would be treated quicker, more efficiently, and more completely if more people were to listen to us and take us seriously.

Emily described another time where, if someone had listened to her, she wouldn't have had such dire outcomes.

"There has been no end of the disbelief of my pain or it's silencing. I often wonder if 'difficult patient' (the dreaded label many chronic pain patients decry when they try to advocate for themselves in a system set up to fail them over and over again) is listed in my medical chart somewhere.

"As recently as five months ago, I had to have my gallbladder removed—a simple, laparoscopic, outpatient surgery. However, I woke up the next day and knew something was terribly wrong. I've had several surgeries in my life (many were more involved than this) and was aware of normal post-op pain. This was nowhere near normal. I went to the ER twice and was sent home after observation with the doctors telling me I was just anxious and constipated.

"My sisters found me nearly unresponsive, gray in color, and unable to communicate two weeks later and took me to the ER for the third time. I had a bile leak, and it had filled my abdomen where I looked seven months pregnant. At the time of this third ER visit, I was in sepsis. They had to do three emergency surgeries to save my life.

"Had they listened to me the first two times and trusted that I knew my body, I wouldn't have had to go through the trauma. And that's exactly what it was—trauma. They had to put in a feeding tube down one nostril, a bile suction tube down the other nostril, cut me open from sternum to pubis to repair tears and wash me out, and put drain tubes in next to my laparotomy incision. I spent two days in the ICU and another nine days in the hospital recovering.

"It is not just medical neglect that we often suffer when medical professionals don't hear us, but the emotional fallout from it all as well. I often wonder how different my mental state would be today if I were listened to, believed, and cared for from the very beginning."

This silencing is, of course, even more egregious in disadvantaged populations in this country, particularly for Black women and other women of color.

In her book, *Invisible Visits: Black Middle-Class Women in the American Healthcare System*, Tina Sacks, an assistant professor of social welfare at UC Berkeley, exposes the statistics about delayed or denied diagnoses and/or treatment and high mortality rates among African Americans.[9]

She states physicians and other medical staff are in some cases even *trained* to treat pain based on racial profiling. She tells us that in one textbook, *Nursing: A Concept-Based Approach to Learning*, first published in 2010, offers advice for nurses when administering pain relief to people from different ethnic backgrounds. It outlines, in depth, how different racial and ethnic groups react differently to acute and chronic pain and uses racist, anti-Semitic, and other stereotypes.

Astonishingly, this is an excerpt from the book:

- Blacks often report higher pain intensity than other cultures. They believe suffering and pain are inevitable.
- Jews may be vocal and demand assistance. They believe pain must be shared and validated by others.
- Hispanics may believe pain is a form of punishment and suffering must be endured . . .

While the publisher has since apologized for the content, it highlights why it isn't surprising that women of color feel silenced, particularly when it comes to chronic pain.

According to the CDC, Black women are three-to-four times more likely to die from pregnancy-related complications than white women. Ana Langer, professor at the Harvard T.H. Chan School of Public Health, thinks a lot of what's happening is medical professionals are not listening to Black women.[10]

"Basically, Black women are undervalued," she says. "They are not monitored as carefully as white women are. When they do present with symptoms, they are often dismissed."

Sheree told me the following about the car accident, which twisted her back for life:

> "Doctors and nurses repeatedly told me 'I was tough' and I didn't need the pain medication. These were not medical professionals who knew me personally, they were first ER doctors, and then clinicians. They had the X-rays and MRIs in front of them. I guessed they were making the assumption I was tough because I was Black. I kept telling them I needed more help, and they kept ignoring me, as if they knew more about what I was feeling than I did."

Of course, one response to this silencing is to rage against the machine. Certainly speaking up and loudly is the only way to change a system that has ingrained bias. But it's not that easy. It's so tiring to live in pain. When we are exhausted, advocating for ourselves feels impossible. Plus, in the end, we need these doctors and other health-care professionals to help us. We don't want to make them angry or agitated. We want them to listen to us, yes, but we also want them to treat us, and sometimes sitting quietly is the only way we can even be present enough to get what we need. We often feel like we'll get better treatment if they like us, so we go out of our way to be friendly, nonconfrontational, and quiet.

We must speak *for each other* as well as speak up for ourselves. When we feel well, we must advocate for health-care professionals to listen and to hear; for fair treatment and allocation of time and resources; and for equity in response and treatment across all demographics. We must convince our partners and families we are not being heard, and yes, we must sometimes depend on them to be our voices when we cannot be our own. We need to know we are not alone in this, and that other women out there understand, empathize, and will fight for our right to be heard.

SHAME

When Humiliation and
Guilt Lead to Defeat

The first time I lost control of my bowels, I was on the platform of the Number 6 train. I was twenty-six, and a cup of coffee I'd sipped led to stomach pain I can only classify as agonizing. Though I did everything I could to get up the subway steps and into a nearby restaurant to relieve it, my cold, shaking body let go three steps from the top.

The problem in a situation like that, I have since learned, is walking makes it worse. And stopping gets you nowhere.

Now covered in a putrid brown film no one could mistake for anything else, I sprinted in shame to my gym, a place that had been my salvation. I rushed into the shower with all my clothes on, peeled them off, pumped bright green body soap into the crotch of my jeans, and threw away my balled-up underwear in a naked dash from the scalding shower to the metal bins.

A young woman wearing a black staff T-shirt shirt approached me in the locker room when I finished my shower. I had seen her many times before, folding towels mostly, mopping the floor, and I always nodded my hello. She always nodded back.

"Are you okay?" she asked.

I was unable to speak.

"Do you want me to wash and dry those for you?" she asked gently, pointing at the heap of wet, smelly clothes on the bench beside me.

I sighed and nodded my thanks and sat in tiny white towels for the next forty-five minutes while this beautiful woman dried my shit-stained clothes.

While the moment remains one of my most humiliating, I think it's important to reflect on the kindness this woman showed me.

She didn't have to help me. She had a lot to do, she was at work, she had a life that did not include cleaning up after me.

We have this assumption that in shameful situations most people will be cruel; they will point and laugh; they will walk away disgusted; and/or they will not help. I'm not sure if that comes from the playground, the horrific news cycle, bad TV, or our own insecurities, but in my experience with shame, it is mostly false.

This example of kindness and help is just one of many I can recount. It is significant because it is one of the first ones.

This woman stopped what she was doing to help me clean up. She looked at me, naked and shaking, sitting next to a pile of wet and dirty clothes that should probably have been thrown out, and she held out her hand to take them. She washed my clothes, and in doing so washed away some of the shame that had covered me, too. Her kindness was a work of grace.

Once they were washed and dried, this kind woman handed me my clothes in a Rite Aid bag someone had left behind. Still shaken into silence, I did a sort of half-bow, which in retrospect was so inadequate, it still haunts me. I put my clothes back on and started the walk home: seventy-three blocks, two avenues and one bridge, just so I didn't have to get on the subway again.

At the time, this was the most humiliating day of my life, (there would be much more humiliation in my future, but I didn't know it yet), and my response was to bury it deep within me. It was only the beginning of the shame I would experience in the next two decades living with a number of autoimmune diseases, which triggered and caused severe, everyday pain and the total breakdown of my body.

Autoimmune disease is a condition in which your body, thinking it is attacking a foreign substance or virus, instead attacks itself. In the case of Crohn's and colitis, this battle takes place in your intestines. Sometimes the pain is mild and occurs after you eat. Other times it is severe and violent, causing your gut to react by trying to expel the food that upsets it as urgently as possible. Crohn's and colitis often present with arthritis of the hips and back, and both diseases are also often married to thyroid malfunction. In thyroid diseases, joints swell and hormones get out of control, causing severe muscular-skeletal pain as well as emotional and mental distress.

Because of the thyroid dysfunction, as well as the humiliation and shame of my daily life, I was left believing I was worthless, my life was a waste, and it was never going to change. I know now that is a hallmark of depression—feeling worthless—but at the time it was new to me. And it felt like an ending.

Nothing else is important when you are in severe pain.

People may say, "Go to work. Stop spending too much money. Eat well. Laugh. Take good care of your children. Be a good wife. Exercise. Chill out."

My mind screams back. *But don't you see what I'm already doing here? Don't you see how hard I'm working just to remain upright? Just to be here?*

And of course they can't see it. Maybe they can see it in my face—the scowl misinterpreted as a bad attitude, a complaint, martyrdom, or pessimism—but they don't see the fire, the ball burning deep in my gut, which demands I pay attention only to it.

I can't blame anyone else for not understanding the pain I feel. I can't blame anyone for inflicting it upon me. I can't blame nature because I realize I am insignificant in the realm of the universe, and I can't blame my life because it has been fortunate in almost every other way.

You see where this is going, of course. If I can't blame any of those things, then the logical place to land the blame is on myself.

Many of us are shamed into a state of defeat. The days stretch and time slows. We lose contact with friends and family. We are alone with the realization that the lives we imagined for ourselves will not be the lives we will live. We realize we cannot get out of this. Women in chronic pain are often on their own, hiding their pain and weakness from a world in which they are met with shame.

I wonder why we feel shame. How does shame change us?

According to Brené Brown, a popular author, lecturer, podcast host, and researcher at the University of Houston, shame is an "intensely painful feeling or experience of believing that we are flawed and therefore unworthy of love and belonging. It's an emotion that affects all of us and profoundly shapes the way we interact in the world. But, depending on how we deal with it, shame can either shut us down or lead us to a new sense of bravery and authenticity."[1]

Brown explains that, "[n]euro-biologically, we're wired above all else for survival, and shame is a threat to connection, a threat to survival. It's very hard to experience shame and not have a very limited response to it. Often shame is a cause of destructive behaviors—self-destructive and violent behaviors towards others. If the fear of shame worked as a deterrent to bad behavior, everyone would be healthy and loving. Instead, shame is highly correlated with things like addiction, depression, violence, and aggression."[2]

Everyone has shame, but for those of us who experience it mostly around our body's malfunction, it seems tangled up in the unfixable reality that is chronic pain.

Every woman I spoke to talked about shame. Without exception, these women had experienced severe shame related to their pain, and some of them were still mired in it.

Jessica, who suffered with scoliosis since she was a teenager, said the following:

"There's shame, embarrassment, and maybe loneliness around the idea that most people in my age range don't deal with chronic pain, and therefore wouldn't understand it. I'm a person who is otherwise very healthy; I'm generally fit and active, so it feels like my chronic pain doesn't fit with how people see me, which makes it hard to acknowledge. And then it feels like a secret. Of course, I'm glad to look and to be generally very healthy, but I wonder if people would hear about my pain and think, 'She doesn't look like she has chronic pain.' It can't be that bad."

I, too, have felt as though my pain should be kept secret. Telling people about it puts an expectation on them that they should care, or more importantly, they should do something to help me. I keep my pain a secret so people don't feel like I'm constantly complaining. I keep quiet because I don't want to be told to.

When my friends and I are out for a glass of wine the one night we have free in a month, they don't need me to bring them down. People always say they don't mind, and it doesn't bother them, but that has to be a lie. Hearing *myself* complain bothers me.

For Katie, who has had stomach pain so severe she was in the hospital for over a month, pain led to an extreme lifestyle change. She had to rework her life, including eating an entirely new, restricted diet, work primarily at home, and generally slow the pace of life and stress as much as possible. But it wasn't just behavioral changes that had to occur. In addition, her mental health, specifically the fear and anxiety around the possibility of getting sick again, played a huge role in her every day. Every time her stomach hurt, she catastrophized the situation, believing she might be headed to the hospital again.

> "I have a lot of PTSD around my hospitalizations—two surgeries, both of which were necessitated by a rapidly escalating condition that would have killed me if left untreated.
>
> "The world struggles enough with the idea of PTSD. PTSD as a medical condition is unbelievable for some people.
>
> "I felt everyone in my life wanted to be past the hospitalization, the fear, the 'overreaction' to stomach pain, but I couldn't move past it. I was scared all the time and I didn't know how not to be. For that, I was deeply ashamed."

Many of us feel a level of guilt around the pressure we put on our loved ones because of our chronic conditions. They have a responsibility to take care of us, and we can often feel as though we are unfairly shackling them to our lives. Maybe the guilt is somewhat warranted. But shame is different from guilt.

Brown explains that the "easiest way to separate shame from guilt is to say shame is, 'I'm bad,' and guilt is, 'I did something bad.' Shame is a focus on self; guilt is a focus on behavior. It's very hard to get out from underneath shame because, if that's who you are, what is the potential for change?"[3]

I think this is especially true in terms of chronic pain. We have something inside of us that, more likely than not, is not going anywhere. The kind of self-perception where we are deficient, broken, or "bad" in some way follows Brown's definition perfectly. If we are "broken" it might be our fault. And if it's our fault, we feel shame around it.

Jessica explains,

"Sometimes, the shame appears in small ways, which snowball into a general sense of weakness and guilt. I can't think of a specific time where shame took over, though I imagine there have been many. I know shame can arise for me when my thoughts make me question my level of responsibility for my pain. *Do my stress and anxiety create the pain? Do I not do enough core exercises? Is my pain tolerance just really low (i.e. am I wimpy)? Would other people just suck it up and push through this level of pain? Am I just being dramatic?"*

There's that feeling of blame again—and the notion that if it is no one else's fault, it must be our own. Sometimes we still have shame, even if those in our orbit do not intensify it. Sometimes, help and love can feel like pity. And pity, once again, feeds this sense of shame.

Jessica goes on,

> "I recognize that I can feel embarrassed or ashamed if a friend who knows about my pain comments that I look physically uncomfortable sometimes. Of course, they mean this with love and care, but it can feel to me like my efforts to cover it up aren't working."

We bury our pain deep under the fabric of our everyday and we think we do a pretty good job of functioning as if we aren't in pain. When someone notices and says something, we realize our effort to hide it is not working. Instead is out in the world for everyone to see.

Maybe there's something to this exposure, though. If we cover up our pain, and subsequently feel shame, which is a manifestation of blaming ourselves, it may be possible that bringing it into the light will help us let go of it.

Emily experiences shame acutely but also explained to me how shame can dissipate the more her suffering is out in the open.

> "For years, I didn't do anything outside of the house because I was in my thirties and used assistive devices. Sadly, I was ashamed and embarrassed at having to use a cane, a walker, or a wheelchair, depending on severity of symptoms. Finally, when I reached forty, I realized I wasn't doing myself any favors, and I also kind of just lost 'giving a fuck' about what others may think. One night, I loaded up my walker into the trunk of my car, headed downtown, and spent the evening rolling from room to room in the Contemporary Art Museum, sitting when I needed to in front of lovely,

thought-provoking artworks, and for the first time in years, felt alive again.

"It's an amazing feeling when shame lifts."

Maybe, as Emily suggests, age and maturity can give us the power we need to squash shame. Maybe we can "stop giving a fuck" and show people what we are actually experiencing without feeling like we put too much expectation and need onto others. I think there are people who can do this, and I think they are brave. But I don't think this works for everyone. I spoke to women well into their sixties about their pain, and many of them have never let go of this sense of intense shame.

Dolores, who has lived with fibromyalgia for over forty years, told me, "When my divorce was final, I sat on the edge of my bed and cried. Because even though I wanted to blame my ex, the truth was, I felt like it was all my fault that we collapsed."

I wonder if, without meaning to, in hiding from the world we are also hiding from each other. What if we all poked our heads out? Maybe we could find some people on the outside can empathize with us. Maybe we can create a community in which we don't have to explain ourselves, we don't have to give too much credence to the "intensely painful feeling or experience of believing we are flawed and therefore unworthy of love and belonging."

Maybe we can all admit we are flawed in the same way. Maybe that's where we'll find our belonging.

PAIN PILLS

The Line Between
Dependency and Addiction

At first, it seems completely reasonable to be taking pain medication to quell pain. That's the point of it, right? The doctor prescribes little white pills. They are so tiny—the size of a ladybug. And they really help. They help more than any other therapy, herb, or medicine available. They are relatively cheap if you have insurance, and they come in a container that fits in your purse. A pharmacist in a professional white lab coat passes them over a counter to you, with a smile that feels like her blessing.

And when you take one, you have a little reprieve—not complete relief, but enough. Sometimes it feels like the pain is wrapped around you . . . still there but padded. Sometimes it gives you time to sleep. Eat. Be present in your life.

Then the pill starts to wear off, and over the weeks and months it's not working as well, and the bottle says you can take one to two for pain. You take two. You tell the doctor you are still in the exact same pain you were in a few weeks or months ago, and he sighs but refills it and through your confused shame, you accept the piece of paper he hands you. And it all happens again. Then suddenly, you wake up and your want has become need.

If it's in the last few years, the next time you go to the same doctor, he has consulted the most recent literature and recommendations from the CDC, FDA, and other health-care authorities who suggest pulling way back on opioid prescriptions and offering alternatives instead.

You try, you really do. You go to therapy week after week and learn to behave the way you want to feel. You wonder when the shift will happen because you are doing everything you are told, and you are still in pain. You go to acupuncture and feel the blood circulating a little better, but the practitioner says it will take a year of biweekly appointments at $150/hour for the pain to retreat. You do an infusion of a new medicine like Cymbalta or Remicade that does alleviate the pain in parts of your body but not in others and comes with a host of dire side effects (including possibly lymphoma). You have to sit for three hours in a hospital every five weeks and take it intravenously. If you don't have sufficient insurance, you get a bill for $16,000 for one infusion.

Perhaps it's a bit better. But it's not *as* better as it was when you took that little ladybug pill. The effort has taken its toll. So maybe you settle on taking the pill again. Maybe you become physically dependent. Maybe the toll it takes on your body is an acceptable trade-off for the toll of your pain. Maybe (albeit a less common occurrence), you become addicted.

What then?

A lot of my pain centers in my stomach, and pain pills are harsh on the intestines. I have never been in a position to become addicted to pain medication. I have taken it. I have loved it. After surgery mostly, or when the arthritis was its angriest. But historically, my body rejects opioids before I can forge an alliance with them, and certainly before I become dependent.

I know what it feels like when you take a pill, and the pain softens. I have had times in my life where I wished I could take them forever. I sometimes wish I had a stomach strong enough to accept the pills so that I could have that kind of relief on a daily basis—the pause in the grind, the moment maybe fifteen minutes after you take the pill, where a sense of cottony calm washes through your blood and you think to yourself, *Oh, right. Life can be like this.*

⎯⎯⎯⎯⎯⎯⎯

The opioid crisis in America is real and devastating. Eighty percent of the world's opioid consumption occurs in the United States. In 2017 alone, opioid drug overdoses killed over 47,000 people.[1] This weighed heavily on me as I wrote this chapter. To be clear, I have respect for and anger about the crushing reality of opioid addiction. The crisis is serious, and the consequences of addiction can be disastrous. But as I was thinking about this, and the relief they offer those of us in pain, I wondered how much of the crisis has to do with appropriately used, prescribed pain killers. How much is caused by people like the women I interviewed for this book?

If opioids didn't hurt my stomach so much, I can say with certainty I would take them more than I should. I might just take them forever. But because I don't know this particular experience, I asked other women in pain about their relationship with pain pills. I got a vast range of responses in terms of addiction, but I got exactly the same response in terms of effect.

So good.

Of course, that's an understatement—so I asked them to elaborate.

"It's like putting a pause on your pain, covering it in gauze, and giving it a break," says Dolores.

It took her twenty-six years to get diagnosed with fibromyalgia and prescribed opioids, so once she was, she wanted to hold on to the relief.

"Once they believed me, I asked for the hard stuff, knowing they might not believe me for long. Nowadays, I squirrel the pills away and only use them when it's completely necessary."

Samantha, who was in the near-fatal riding incident, explained that with pain medication, the "temporary absence of feeling—any feeling—has come as sweet relief."

On our video call to discuss pain meds and addiction, Adele leaned back in her chair, the first smile of our conversation curling her lips.

"It's the only thing that helps," she said, without prompting.

But while most of the women I spoke to agreed opiods like Vicodin, Percocet, OxyContin, and fentanyl soften their ever-present pain, they had different responses when I asked them about dependency and addiction.

Here's the difference between addiction and dependence, a distinction I have learned about only recently, according to the National Institute on Drug Abuse.

Physical dependence is when the body adapts to the drug, requiring more of it to achieve a certain effect (tolerance) and eliciting drug-specific physical or mental symptoms if drug use is abruptly ceased (withdrawal). Physical dependence can happen with the chronic use of many drugs, including many prescription drugs, even if taken as instructed.[2]

Addiction (or compulsive drug use despite harmful consequences) is characterized by an inability to stop using a drug;

failure to meet work, social, or family obligations; and some-times (depending on the drug), tolerance and withdrawal.[3]

Thus, physical dependence by itself does not constitute addiction, but it often accompanies addiction. This distinction can be difficult to discern, particularly with prescribed pain medications, for which the need for increasing dosages can represent tolerance or a worsening underlying problem, as opposed to the beginning of abuse or addiction.[4]

Loss of control, usage despite knowing the harm, preoccupation, and insatiable craving, all signal addiction to pain medication. Rivermend Health Center is a leading facility that specializes in treating drug and alcohol addiction, dual disorders, and pain medication abuse. According to the center, "Almost all patients who use an opioid pain medication like fentanyl, hydrocodone, morphine, oxycodone, Oxycontin, and Dilaudid for more than a month will experience physical withdrawal symptoms (dependence) when they stop taking the medication." Research suggests the majority of people who become addicted to prescription opioids actually *don't* obtain them from a doctor, but use and misuse medication prescribed to family or friends.

The research shows it *isn't* primarily those who are being treated for chronic pain who are becoming addicted. The National Institution on Drug Abuse states that only ". . . between 8 and 12% of people using an opioid for chronic pain develop an opioid use disorder (addiction)."[5]

This means that 88–92% of people prescribed opioids for chronic pain do *not* get addicted. Most people can miss this important distinction. I think most people believe if they take pain medicine for a long time, they will become addicted. That's what I always thought. You may become tolerant (meaning you need more and more of the drug to treat the pain), and you may become dependent (you may experience withdrawal if you stop taking it). But thinking if you take pain medication to treat chronic pain you are heading toward a lifetime of addiction isn't true. Everything I read tells me opioids become less effective over time, necessitating higher doses in order to treat the same level of pain.

But that did not pan out in the conversations I had. Many of the women I talked to have been taking pain medicine for years, and for a couple of them, decades. Many of them have taken the same prescribed dose they always have.

They feel they work, and work better than any alternative. Are they experiencing a trick of the mind? Are they responding to something other than pain relief? Is it medically impossible that these drugs at stable doses have been helping them for this long? I don't know. But, if they aren't addicted (meaning, they aren't misusing their prescription with the intention of getting high, or ruining their relationships, or holding the pills above all else) maybe it doesn't matter. If it isn't damaging them, who are we to say what's too much?

Opioids are getting harder to procure. Currently, they are mostly prescribed for acute, temporary pain, and doctors are wary of prescribing them for anything long-term. Trish Randall, a chronic pain sufferer and long-term opioid user wrote about her experience with the regulatory system in *Filter*. "Being a long-term, high-dose opioid patient means living under a suspected-murderer level of scrutiny . . . The patient must adhere to conditions like paper prescriptions only, no phone-ins; an in-person appointment every twenty-eight days; and urine tests and pill counts at any or all appointments or on twenty-four hours notice any time I receive a call. Only one doctor and one pharmacy can handle the prescriptions. Other conditions can include no cigarettes, alcohol, or illegal drugs (on the theory that pain patients must be discouraged from sliding into addiction), and being required to attend psychiatric or psychological appointments."[6]

There has been a deluge of information in the past few years about the opioid crisis and the dire effects it is having on our society. But this focus on addiction seems to have confused the conversation for chronic pain sufferers. I'm not arguing the opioid crisis is not a monumental problem that must be addressed. But this focus has made it difficult for chronic pain patients to get the medication they need to manage their pain. Doctors no longer want to prescribe long term. Society now casts significant judgment on those who use pain medication chronically. It's also a lot harder to get the drugs. Because of this, some people in chronic pain are turning to street drugs like off-market opioids and illegal counterparts with similar effect. Clearly, these unregulated versions are much more dangerous.

As Randall points out, "Thanks to blanket media coverage of the opioid-involved overdose crisis—which, while devastating, affects only a tiny proportion of all who use opioids, mostly people who are not prescribed these drugs and combine them with other substances—many Americans have a hugely inflated sense of opioids' ability to get you hooked, and to kill."[7]

Katie MacBride is a journalist and an expert on addiction and the-ever changing regulations and restrictions levied on opioids. Her piece in *Healthline*, "Restricting Opioids Doesn't Prevent Addiction. It Just Harms People Who Need Them," has been integral in helping me understand this landscape.

She also had a lot to say when I spoke with her one-on-one. To be as transparent and clear as possible, when I quote her from an interview, I am calling her "Katie," with only her first name, like the other women I quote from conversations. When I have quoted from her work, I'm calling her "MacBride," to be sure she gets the credit she is definitely due.

Katie is a pain sufferer, with severe stomach pain and migraines, and she had this to say when I asked her about the difference between dependence and addiction:

"I think there's a lot of confusion about the difference between being dependent on a drug and having a substance use disorder. I absolutely think we should have acceptance around being dependent on medication. For some medications, we already are accepting of that. You don't see people criticizing diabetics for being dependent on insulin. I don't know why you'd criticize someone for being dependent on opioids to manage pain. We shouldn't criticize anyone for having a substance use disorder, either, but in my opinion, it's fair to say ideally someone gets treatment for a SUD and that's not typically required for simply being dependent on a medication.

"Substance use disorders (SUDs) are a range of stages where one is 'misusing' substances, or using them with the expressed purpose of getting high. These can range from severe—what we typically think of as addiction—to disorders of less severity, where people are not necessarily using them with the type of compulsivity and escalation, resulting in negative consequences more characteristic of addiction. I personally believe we need massive de-stigmatization efforts around drug users and people with SUDs, but I don't know that it's necessarily related to chronic (physical) pain.

"Typically, SUDs consist of taking medication beyond what is needed to address the physical pain. I think we need to seriously broaden our horizons about drugs and medications that can treat both physical pain and mental health disorders, but once you get into SUDs, you're past what is needed strictly to address those issues."

I've admitted I was not clear on this medical distinction prior to researching this book, but it's critical. The idea that all those who are physically dependent have an addiction problem is wrong.

Katie says,

"The thing that I find so absurd about restricting pain medication for patients with chronic pain is that we know that opioid prescriptions for patients with chronic pain aren't the major driver behind opioid addiction."

Those with opioid addiction rarely have been prescribed the medicine for chronic pain. Instead, they often use other people's prescriptions and take the pills not to quell pain, but to get high. Restricting opioid use for chronic pain sufferers does not address this.

"It's just an ineffective solution to the problem and extremely harmful to boot,"[8] MacBride says.

I didn't know if the other women I spoke to recognized this distinction between dependence and addiction, either. It may be possible that those who consider themselves addicted might actually just be dependent.

I asked the women if they experienced any of the below indicators of addiction:

- Take a higher dose than prescribed
- Take someone else's prescription, even for a legitimate problem, like pain
- Take it to get high
- Find yourself preoccupied with the drug and when you're next scheduled to take it[8]

Two out of the eleven women I asked agreed they found themselves with one of the above characteristics. The rest felt confident they were taking the medication as was prescribed to them, at the right dose, at the right time, to manage their incessant pain.

Because the differences between addiction and dependence are not well understood or recognized, the people in our lives can have similar judgments of both. The predominant opinion is that taking pain pills for a long time means you are addicted to them. Whether or not that's true, it can feel like by taking the pills we are disappointing people, disgusting people, or letting them down. This makes us feel like treating our pain is a weakness, but we don't see another way out.

When we're drowning, we grab for the life jacket, because the life jacket promises to save our life. We want to survive.

Of course, for some, opioids don't only quiet pain, and maybe that's where the problem lies. The attachment that grows is not only to the numbing, which is why opioids can be so dangerous. The addiction can also be to the way the world starts to soften, and things once horrible feel more manageable. The pills may or may not be treating the pain any longer, but they are making the world less harsh, which, in turn, makes the pain a little less harsh, too.

This is where things can get dangerous. This is where, for some of the women I interviewed, things can spiral.

When Samantha started taking her prescribed opioids, addiction was far from her mind.

She said,

> "I didn't start taking pills for recreation or to check out of my life. I took it for physical suffering. The line into addiction starts to blur. These opioids don't only alleviate aches in the body. There is a numbness, a wrapped-in-cotton sensation that allows you to function but be protected from the sharpness of life."

For Katie, risk of addiction was always too high.

> "I used to take Vicodin for my migraines, but it only sort of helped. I didn't have any qualms about being a recovering alcoholic taking Vicodin because at best Vicodin was only 25% effective and 0% as fun as drinking. My doctors knew my history of addiction and thus had never offered Oxy for migraines. I wouldn't take it, anyway. If I was in constant pain, I would consider it, but knowing I'd have a break from the pain in a few days didn't seem worth the risk. I knew too many people in rehab who were there because of Oxy. It just seems like unnecessarily playing with fire."

As someone with a history of addiction, Katie is not willing to take the chance, but what about the other women I spoke to who did not have a history?

Sheree's serious car accident in 2011 had left her spine forever curved in a "C" shape. Sitting is excruciating. She works an office job where she is at a desk at least eight hours a day.

She has two children, one of whom still likes to be picked up and carried around. Her husband travels most weeks, and along with full-time work, she is responsible for all after-school activities as well as most of the house duties (laundry, cooking, cleaning etc.).

She was prescribed Oxycontin for eighteen months after the accident, only to be cut off by weaning her down to nothing when the doctor decided she'd had enough. Guidelines stated that over time, doctors should offer fewer prescriptions for fewer days and at lower dosages.

Sheree admits to seeing different prescribers to keep her supply current.

"I'm not lying, really," she said, "but I don't always tell them how long ago the accident was, and I don't always share how many other doctors have prescribed it. I feel awful about it, but at this point it feels like I just need it. It makes me feel like I can actually function in my life."

This dance has proven more difficult to choreograph lately, something Sheree fears will be a new norm.

When I asked her if she considered herself an addict, she paused.

"I guess I'm dependent, in that if I don't have it my body reacts. I sweat, I get irritable, and I hurt. But I take thyroid medication, hormones, and antidepressants. I feel pretty bad when I don't take those, too. Look at the lists of side effects on those. I don't see how this is any different. I'm in pain. This helps. It's my medicine. I don't abuse it. I use it as it's intended. End of story."

MacBride reminds us, "The thing is, we already have tons of restrictions on opioid prescriptions, but there's no indication they're preventing addiction and every indication they're hurting chronic pain patients."[9]

My reaction is one of empathy, mainly. In my everyday life, I take about twelve pills daily, a three-hour infusion every five weeks, and enough supplements to kill a horse. Sure, my medications are not pain pills, but they are strong and have serious side effects. I am without a doubt dependent. Without my pills and IVs, I am quite sick, in horrible pain, and in an extreme scenario, I could die. How is this different? If they cut my infusions off because some people were becoming addicted to it, how would I get through my days?

As dutiful patients, we want to do what's right. We try the alternatives the doctor orders in place of the pain medication we have come to love. We accept that addiction to opioids is bad for us, and maybe it's just that we aren't trying hard enough. Maybe with enough effort, some of these alternatives might actually work.

A report by the CDC in 2017 outlined some of the alternatives to opioid pain medication that doctors have adopted. The primary alternatives are outlined as follows:

1. CBT (cognitive behavior therapy)
2. Exercise
3. Nonopioid, pharmacologic approaches
4. Acetaminophen
5. NSAIDs like ibuprofen
6. Anticonvulsants
7. Interventional approaches, such as epidural injection[10]

I read the list of alternatives to some of the women I interviewed. All of them laughed, just as I did when I first read it.

The pain they live in was so severe—fibromyalgia, migraines, stomach disease, life-altering injuries, degenerative arthritis, connective tissue disease, and facial nerve disease—that *not one* woman felt any of the suggested alternatives came close to the relief offered by pain medication. Collectively, they had tried them all, even medical marijuana for pain, which is not on the CDC's alternatives list because in certain states it is still considered a Schedule 1 (illegal) drug.

When I asked her about medical grade marijuana, Adele, a sixty-eight-year-old woman with rheumatoid arthritis, told me it made her a bit calmer, but didn't touch the pain.

Adele has been in constant back, knee, and hip pain for the past thirty-plus years. She has tried every other therapy out there. She tried CBD and THC when friends told her it helped them with their more everyday pain.

"The calm is nice for a couple of hours, but the pain stays the same, for the most part. I have to sort of smile and nod vaguely when friends ask me if it helps. I don't want to be rude, but I think to myself their pain must be a joke if they think this helps."

Katie told me:

"As an alternative, I got a medical cannabis prescription, which has helped, though not as directly as you might think. I think the CBD has helped with stress, which decreases the frequency of stress-induced migraines. I'll use THC when I have a migraine, but mostly because it puts me to sleep. Sleeping is the only way I've found to really get rid of a migraine."

Samantha said,

"My solution has been to take advantage of therapies when I can, but otherwise accept that I will live with a slow, dull pain much of the time."

There it is again. The idea of acceptance.

Not everyone agrees pills are more harmful than helpful. In terms of the women I spoke to who still take pain pills daily, do they consider themselves addicts?

Two of the women feel they can, and do, take breaks from the medication, noting they know the long-term risks of the medications must be tempered. But the others—they simply don't care.

"This is me," Adele said. "Take it or leave it."

Some of the others had similar responses. If people think they live a life of dependence or consider them addicts, they accept it. They feel they have no other choice, and it is nobody's business. Adele told me:

"Look, I won't say there's no shame. My friends and family don't know the extreme extent of my dependence but neither can they understand the intensity of my pain. It's mine. It's horrible. I get through the day with my pills. Those are mine, too. They can rip them out of my cold dead hands."

Of course, responses and experiences are varied. Some people who take pain medication become addicted, some don't. But if we believe that acceptance of our medical conditions is possible in the trenches of chronic pain, I wonder, *Is there a place for the acceptance of long-term opioid dependence, too?*

Samantha didn't think so. When I asked her if she could imagine a world in which she would go back on pain pills and accept a certain form of long-term need, she had this to say:

"Chronic pain for me is this gnawing ache. I sometimes imagine it literally as a tiny creature gnawing on my leg. Not enough to kill me, just enough to make me permanently distracted. Or sometimes I think of it like a leech, slowly draining my life force and making me exhausted all the time. But would I ever go back on painkillers? I think about that. I can tell you that the few times in the past years when I have had them—postdental surgery and once after a gallbladder operation—the temporary absence of feeling, any feeling, has come as sweet relief. But then I remember the tunnel that leads to the depression, the hopelessness, the selfishness, and the harm it can cause to the people who love you. My body so quickly adjusts to dosages that the relief is never more than momentary, and everything comes crashing back. Is there a world in which I could accept addiction, though? I don't think so. Not because I don't like the fantasy of it but because I know the reality."

We cannot ignore what Samantha and others state. Opioids are not like other drugs that have frightening side effects. This class of drugs can grab us and make us want more and more, until we depend on them for more than just pain management.

There's really no way to know how you will react until you do, which may be too risky a proposition for some.

But a path to addiction doesn't seem to be true for everyone I spoke to, and it isn't a forgone conclusion in the research, either. Many women in pain do not tunnel into the depths of depression or ruin their relationships or their lives. Women like Sheree and Adele manage their pain with medication and are able to function in their everyday life. Sheree would say she can function better *because* of it. Many people go on living the best they can, taking their daily pills like all the other medication they have to take, keeping the pain at bay.

Which leads me to what I'm sure will be a controversial question: If we remove the judgment from this kind of dependence (that which many of us think of as addiction), let go of shame, can we as a society accept this?

There are serious implications to this kind of acceptance. I'm sure there are many people who would find even this suggestion cavalier, foolish, or dangerous. I have lost some beautiful people to outright addiction. If people who do not need to control pain overuse or become dependent or addicted to pain pills, this would be a different scenario. But if pain medicine helps alleviate pain more successfully than the alternatives, and women in pain feel they need it and it *doesn't* upend their lives, who gets to decide if it's worth it?

There are, of course, long-term, detrimental, physical side effects of being on opioids, particularly high doses. The US National Library of Medicine says that, "[O]pioid therapy can adversely affect respiratory, gastrointestinal, musculoskeletal, cardiovascular, immune, endocrine, and central nervous systems."[11]

All of this can be severe, sometimes even fatal. But common, over-the-counter medications can have serious side effects, too. Even ibuprofen can have serious, adverse side effects, including gastrointestinal, renal, cardiovascular, cerebrovascular, and central nervous system adverse effects.

Of course, long-term opioid use can be severely detrimental. But who gets to decide what risks we are willing to take? How much of our own lives do we get to control? With all of the medication prescribed to us on a daily basis and all of the possible side effects (including death) listed on many of the bottles, this doesn't feel much different. If we believe these women and their analyses of the alternatives offered—and I think we should—their experience is what ought to drive our collective understanding of chronic pain and the access to the pain medication used to manage it.

MENTAL ILLNESS

The Link Between Our Minds
and Our Bodies

The smell of the mental hospital hit me quickly. The Crohn's disease and thyroid cancer I experienced in my twenties left me physically ransacked and chronically ill. I've stayed in many medical hospitals, and somehow the sharp scent of antiseptic always calms me down. The scent of the medical jolt of an IV flush that flies through the air softens my nerves. It says, "hospital" to me. It says someone is about to help me.

This place did not smell sharp and clean like a hospital. It didn't smell dirty or bad, not the way I imagine it could—the body odor of everyone's discontent marinating in the corners of the carpet. It smelled like a musty basement . . . a room closed up for too long.

There were coloring books on the tables. Thick, juicy markers and those with very fine points. Mandalas. Sudokus. Word searches. A teenage boy who looked like a high school football player scribbled hurriedly in green Cray-Pas over an Apples to Apples box. He looked up when I came in and didn't smile.

"You want a Cray-Pas?" he asked. "You can have any one but green."

I shook my head no.

The next morning, I had breakfast with a woman who was trying to peel the skin off her neck, and lunch with a woman eating her lettuce with her two fingers, dipping it into her decaf tea and slurping the hot lettuce liquid. At dinner I sat next to a woman who picked her nose and wiped her lips with it.

They took the elastic from my sweatpants, the razor from my shower kit, the cell phone from my purse, and the laces from my shoes.

One woman couldn't sleep until she had read the whole paper backward. One man told me he tried to choke himself to death the night before with a pillowcase.

People wore ironically happy clothes. Neon flannel pajama pants with pink ribbons. Smiley face T-shirts. The sweatshirts had hoods, but none had drawstrings.

How did all this start where I ended up here? It started when I told someone I didn't think I deserved to live. That person brought me to the emergency room, and I said, "I can't feel anything anymore. Nothing brings me joy like it used to."

It was decided I belonged somewhere safe. They stationed someone as a guardian in front of my ER stall to make sure I didn't find a way out.

The second guard who stayed with me was a heavyset woman with a thick wooden cross bouncing against her bosom. She wore a quilted leather bag on her arm. The nurse left my side and squeaked down the hall, a flowered perfume in her wake. The guard pretended to take her seat. When the coast was clear, though, she shot up. She charged toward my bed, where I was curled up and shaking, unable to stop crying.

"You have children?" she asked.

"Yes."

"A husband?"

"Yes."

"They need you."

"I know."

"You love them?"

"More than I ever thought possible."

"OK, then you let Jesus in your heart. That's it; you'll be good as new. Let Jesus in."

I didn't reply.

She didn't relent.

"This depression. This is your fault. You let the devil in."

I said nothing.

With a finger in my face, she said it again. "You let the devil in your soul."

I didn't know if the devil was in there or not. I didn't know if I let him in. But I did know for absolute sure that just deciding to believe something I have never believed before would not fix this. I was quite sure that nothing could. Definitely not Jesus.

I sank further into my heated cotton sheet and shut my eyes, willing her to turn away.

Thankfully, the nurse came back down the hall, her sneaker squeak announcing her arrival. And with a few signed papers and careful nods, I was transferred to the mental hospital.

I should back up, though. It had been two years that I had been severely depressed. Maybe an extension of postpartum depression, though we'll never know, possibly thyroid related, because I didn't have one.

I didn't even really know I was depressed myself. I didn't connect the not being able to do anything all day—not being able to pick up the phone, not being able to tolerate the reality of chronic disease and the pain, not being able to feel joy, not sleeping, overeating, shopping too much—with anything serious.

I wish people understood depression is not sadness. I imagine it's pretty individual, but here's what it is for me. It's the tips of my fingers vibrating because the air feels ice cold to the touch. It's a blank mind that tumbles into a mind full of doubt—about reality, worth, and love. It's not missing the beauty in life. It's feeling it too much. It's feeling that if I look too closely at a child, at the ocean, at a little bud on the end of a branch, it just might crack me open. It's an empty chest. It's being bone tired. It's the monster under my bed. It's around every corner. It could be the answer to every question I'm too afraid to ask. It is quick breath. It is the edge of something real and deep and dark and relentless. It is reaching the core of myself—of the world or reality or darkness—and finding out that what's there is not what I'd hoped would be there. Instead of the burning fire I expected, all that's there is a deep, cold, well.

Here's what my depression feels like: My stomach is on the floor. My heart beats fast, but I can't move. Everything is impossible to accomplish. Something as easy as brushing my teeth, packing my kids' lunch boxes, or sending an email seems out of the realm of possibility.

It is feeling nothing connected with feeling everything. That's what's so hard to explain. The sensitivity is so acute, it is like I could ignite a spark by the tentacles of my nerve endings. My heart is on the outside, my back tensed and curved to protect it. It doesn't mean that the fiery love I have for my children and my husband is gone, or I feel any differently deep down about my loved ones—my family, who has always been unwaveringly good to me and my friends who know me sometimes better than I know myself. It's almost the opposite. Those loves, those emotions have gotten so intense, I can't take it anymore. All I can do is turn that feeling inside out and bury it far down inside my core so that it doesn't hurt so much. If I'm able to accomplish that, I can zombie through the day, numb, closed, and afraid. Everything is an enormous challenge. These mundane things are still almost impossible to achieve. And then, finally, I can't pretend anymore; I can't move any more. And my bed is my only salvation.

That's where things get dangerous. I can sometimes feel that without a doubt, a world in which people didn't have to take care of me all the time would be better for everyone. (I know this is not true now.) Even when I have depressive episodes now, I know it.

I'm pretty sure I knew it intellectually, then. But emotionally, I believed in my worthlessness completely. When my brain is in that kind of depression, all that makes sense is full erasure. I don't know if being in pain led to my depression, or if my depression led to my pain, or if they are simply manifestations of the same thing. One thing I do know is that since getting on antidepressants and mood stabilizers and seeing a very wonderful therapist *a lot*, I have less depression. But I do not have less pain. So the connection, while plausible, does not entirely hold up.

If I don't treat my depression, I cannot stand the pain, which is a problem. I do what I can to "feel" better . . . to "think" better . . . to "be" better. It is a struggle I fight every single day.

One of the most difficult realities of chronic pain as it relates to depression is the discrepancies in the medical field about the connection and what to do about it.

In *The Link between Depression and Chronic Pain: Neural Mechanisms in the Brain*, researchers explore this connection.

"Their coexistence tends to further aggravate the severity of both disorders. Unfortunately, their association remains unclear, which creates a bottleneck problem for managing chronic, pain-induced depression. In recent years, studies have found considerable overlaps between pain- and depression-induced neuroplasticity changes and neurobiological mechanism changes. Such overlaps are vital to facilitating the occurrence and development of chronic pain and chronic pain-induced depression." [1]

Because this was new to me, I looked up the definition of neuroplasticity and neurobiological mechanism.

Neuroplasticity refers to the lifelong capacity of the brain to change and rewire itself in response to the stimulation of learning and experience. Neurogenesis is the ability to create new neurons and connections between neurons throughout a lifetime.

Our brains change over time, which we know because we are constantly proactively learning, but they also change without our control. If the neuroplasticity and neurobiological mechanism of both depression and pain do overlap, then it makes sense that one exists as the other develops. This is not to say that everyone with chronic pain has mental illness, but it does indicate mental illness is a neurobiological reaction, just like physical pain. Depression and other mental illnesses should be considered a physical reaction, as opposed to being "all in our heads."

I asked women about their relationship with mental illness as it related (or didn't relate) to their physical pain. Many of them had experiences like mine, though most were not as severe.

Katie, who suffers from severe stomach pain and struggles with anxiety on a daily basis, feels that mental and physical pain are yoked where one no longer exists without the other.

She told me:

"They are inextricably linked. My month-long hospitalization during which I had two colon surgeries was the most physically painful experience of my life. That kind of pain is deeply traumatic; it's a constant, blinding reminder of how close I came to death (and how close I still am). It's also incredibly lonely; no one else truly understands what you're feeling."

Not everyone who experiences chronic physical pain also experiences mental illness, but many do. About 50% of people who have chronic pain also have depression.

Harvard Health further explained, "People with chronic pain have three times the average risk of developing psychiatric symptoms—usually mood or anxiety disorders—and depressed patients have three times the average risk of developing chronic pain."[2]

Dolores has struggled with fibromyalgia as well as bipolar depression for decades.

She said, "I don't see a difference between mental pain and physical pain. I hurt because I hurt."

There are always biological, genetic, and situational reasons for mental illness, especially depression. However, for chronic pain sufferers, the catalyst is often the physical pain. We hurt. We can't explain it. It never eases up. We get angry with our friends and family who are free to live comfortably. We drown in fear and worry about the next diagnosis that will make things even harder. We crave the life we once lived. We become positive we have done something to deserve our suffering. We tumble into the dark well of depression, and our bodies are not strong enough to help us get out.

Kate deals with acute trauma and PTSD from her experience with TN.

"It has been over ten years since I lived with TN pain. And I'm still trying to unpack all of the anguish and trauma living with that kind of pain creates. When you google trigeminal neuralgia, the first words you see are, 'the suicide disease.' I saw that on day one. I understand why it is called that. But no one without TN can understand it. It's not possible to describe or empathize with the kind of pain TN creates. Immediately you're put in a very lonely, very dark hole."

In Samantha's case, mental illness is at the heart of her struggle, and it is married to the silence she imparts around her pain.

She told me:

"[f]or the most part, I keep my challenges to myself. I express my struggles with depression and addiction with very, very few people. For those who look closely, though, I always think it evident, undergirding all my work. And yes, depression at least is a physical weight that lives in the body."

While treating depression may be helpful for addressing chronic pain, there *are* instances in which mental illness is used as an excuse to ignore the physical, which can be dangerous as well. Depression and pain can be linked, and they are in my case, but it is important not to lump them together across the board.

For Emily, depression stood in the way of a diagnosis for a long time. She told me the following:

"After I became bedridden by my pain, I saw a therapist to help me deal with the new challenges the pain brought. I was also immensely sad that I had to leave my son for a time, so I would often cry. Many doctors used this as evidence that my pain stemmed from depression and dismissed my complaints. I spent two years telling doctors that my hips hurt and that I could barely walk. I pleaded with them to investigate further before they finally decided to send me for X-rays.

"When they received the results, they gasped and said that I had the hips of an eighty-five-year-old woman (I was thirty-two at the time). I had to have both hips replaced by age thirty-five because of multiple issues, the least of which was depression.

"[Which comes first, physical or mental pain] is an interesting question, and it's a very chicken or the egg situation. Meaning, I'm not convinced one way or another. I've dealt with situational depression at times in my life and I had what was labeled 'anxiety' for years, only to find out I had a heart condition. So I feel a lot of ways about it all.

"I know that if you have depression or anxiety written anywhere in your health records, you are almost guaranteed to be told your pain is because of those things and offered an antidepressant. In my personal experience, nothing moved the dial for me more than getting off antidepressants. Again, that's my own experience and I wouldn't tell anyone or advise them unless you have a plan and support system in place."

I understand what Emily is saying, but for me, living in the endless cycle of this kind of chicken and egg can make things immeasurably worse, and finding a way to quiet the mental illness is as much a part of my treatment as any physical answer.

I always felt like I *felt* more. Emotionally speaking, I'm extremely sensitive. It has been a weakness in my life—people have taken advantage of me.

When I was a child, I didn't always understand when people were cruel. I cried longer than I should have when things went wrong.

It has also been a strength. I can tell when people are upset just from the air in the room. I can ask the right questions in stressful situations, and I can make people feel comfortable when they are otherwise upset. I am very empathetic.

There has been a slew of research in the past few years about empathy and the brain. Interestingly, there is new evidence that the areas of the brain connected to physical pain are also the origins of empathy. Does that mean that feeling things both physically and emotionally is the same thing? If so, what does that mean for chronic pain and mental health?

In his 2017 piece, *Where Empathy Lives in the Brain*, Deepa Padmanaban tells us, "Psychologists call this vital skill 'theory of mind,' or the ability to attribute thoughts and beliefs to others. Theory of mind is what makes us aware of our own selves and what distinguishes us from others and helps us understand that others can experience the world differently from the way we do. It's the reason you can understand what someone is thinking and anticipate what they're going to do or say next."[3]

My experience is that I have a heightened ability to attribute thoughts and beliefs (and feelings) to others based on very little information. Sometimes it is the tilt of their head or a phrase that clues me in. Sometimes it's as subtle as the energy in the room. When people talk about empaths, they are talking about me.

I'm not alone in this. Many of the women I spoke to also have noticed this heightened sense of empathy in themselves. Kate told me the following:

"I was always a sensitive person but living with chronic pain made me infinitely more empathetic. I would now describe myself as an empath. I can't take in media that I know will upset me, unless I'm feeling strong enough. I think this process is partly due to just living with an 'invisible' amount of pain and the understanding that anyone and potentially everyone has a certain level of it. But living with pain also made me so appreciative of others' empathy toward me. There were people who were very good at helping in tiny ways and now that I am on the other side of living with pain, all I want is to be that helper."

An international team led by researchers at Mount Sinai School of Medicine in New York "has for the first time shown that one area of the brain, called the anterior insular cortex, is the only activity center of human empathy, whereas other areas of the brain are not."[4]

In the study, "Does Rejection Hurt?" Naomi I. Eisenberger et. al. demonstrate that these regions were activated when people experienced an experimental social rejection from peers. In another study, the same regions were activated when people who had recently broken up with romantic partners viewed pictures of the former partner.[5]

Alan Fogel, in his 2017 *Psychology Today* piece, "Emotional and Physical Pain Activate Similar Brain Regions; Where

Does Emotion Hurt in the Body?" suggests what I have been wondering about—should we be treating mental illness with physical pain remedies?

He asks, "If physical and emotional pain have similar neural signatures, why not take Tylenol (acetaminophen) for grief, loss, or despair?

"In one study, people who had experienced a recent social rejection were randomly assigned to take acetaminophen vs. a placebo daily for three weeks. The people in the acetaminophen condition reported fewer hurt feelings during that period. When their brains were scanned at the end of the treatment period, the acetaminophen takers had less activation in the anterior insula and the anterior cingulate cortex.

"This study was not done in order to promote acetaminophen and other analgesics as psychoactive drugs. Rather, the idea was to emphasize that over the course of evolution, our bodies decided to take the economic route and use a single neural system to detect and feel pain, regardless of whether it is emotional or physical. While it may be a good idea to take a pain reliever in the acute phase of feeling physical and emotional pain, no one is proposing this as a long-term cure for dealing with hurt feelings and grief."[6]

———•———•———

Of course, to those of us who live in chronic pain, these findings are not shocking. I'm not the only one who has always felt more empathetic than those around me.

Sheree said:

"I know it sounds insane, but I have always felt like I knew what people around me were feeling before they did. It's a feeling, you know? Maybe a superpower. I'll tell you, it makes life harder, because I'm always absorbing other people's sadness."

Jessica hadn't made the link explicitly, but when I asked about whether she felt empathy and pain might be connected, it rang true for her.

"I don't know about this, but I am definitely more emotionally sensitive than lots of others I know. I also feel I grew up with the word 'sensitive' having a negative connotation, and I've been labeled as 'too sensitive' at times. I'm a person who, from an emotional perspective, feels things deeply and intensely. And as I write about this, I notice my brain automatically wants to self-blame—i.e., 'I'm so overly sensitive that I overreact to my pain . . . I make my pain worse because I'm sensitive . . . the anxiety and stress I experience exacerbate my pain . . . so my pain is my fault.'

"But I also know that in lots of areas, including my career as a therapist and my relationships, my sensitivity is a valuable strength. Interestingly, I haven't considered that maybe my physical pain has contributed to my ability to be sensitive and empathic to the emotional pain of others, but now I can see that it probably has."

What used to be considered unlikely—that it is possible to physically feel someone else's pain just by watching it—has recently been proven.

According to Charles Q. Choi in his 2017 *LiveScience* piece, "People Literally Feel Pain of Others," he states, "A brain anomaly can make the saying, 'I know how you feel' literally true in hyperempathetic people who actually sense that they are being touched when they witness others being touched. The condition, known as mirror-touch synesthesia, is related to the activity of mirror neurons, cells recently discovered to fire not only when some animals perform some behavior, such as climbing a tree, but also when they watch another animal do the behavior. For 'synesthetes,' it's as if their mirror neurons are on overdrive. Now scientists find these synesthetes possess an unusually strong ability to empathize with others."[7]

Dr. Jamie Ward, University College London cognitive neuroscientist, explains this further. "We often flinch when we see someone knock their arm, and this may be a weaker version of what these synesthetes experience."[8]

I have always had a physical response to seeing blood, particularly when it is connected to violence. I physically recoil when someone on screen is shot, and even more when they are cut or tortured in any way. I know most people feel disgust and maybe even fear when they witness this, but when I asked around about the specific physical reactions people had in these types of scenarios, I was shocked most people didn't experience them physically. I get weak in the knees. My stomach wrenches, and I get dizzy and faint. Some people I talked to have this reaction, too. But I also feel the specific pain (although clearly not as severely) in the place on the body where the victim is attacked. If they are cut in the throat, I feel pain in my throat. If they chop a hand off, my wrist hurts. It isn't just a fear or stressed-based reaction. It is a synesthete one. I never considered this to be abnormal. Until reading the research on it, I had never paid attention to this relationship between what I see others experience and what I physically feel myself. I was shocked most people I talked to (outside of those I interviewed about pain) did not connect to this experience.

Machael Banissy, a doctoral student who works with Ward, told *LiveScience*, ". . . when we observe another person being touched, we all activate areas of our brain similar to those activated when we are physically touched. In mirror-touch synesthetes, this mirror system is overactive. The resulting high level of empathy they demonstrate supports the notion that people learn to empathize by putting themselves in someone else's shoes.

"It is extraordinary to think that some people experience touch on their own body when they merely watch someone else being stroked or punched. However, this may be an exaggeration of a brain mechanism that we all possess to some degree," Ward said.[9]

Adele might not know the science behind it, but she understands it innately. She told me, "I hurt more because I hurt more; I feel more because I feel more. I never thought it was strange."

Maybe this research can give doctors and other medical professionals new ways to look at their chronic pain patients. Maybe it can give mental health providers something to work with, too. Perhaps if we feel more emotionally, and this is connected to us feeling more physically, treating one could address the other. It could be imperative that a person in chronic pain also see a psychiatrist. We could put aside some of the stigma we have around mental illness and look at the brain's reactions as more data in our quest to help those in physical pain. We could look at the body as a whole picture, instead of isolating hips, or backs or nerves or brains. This research gives us the freedom to explore the idea that if we treat one, we might be also treating the other and it seems like enormous progress.

FAT

Overweight and Underdiagnosed

I weigh 165 pounds. I am five feet tall. People are shocked by this. It is heavier than many of my friends who are much taller than I am. I am also dense—as my children are—so I imagine, in some ways, it's genetic. I look a little less heavy than I am. But people still see fat when they see me. I am on the obesity scale at the doctor's office. When I was pregnant, I was over 200 pounds. Again, I'm very short, so this is a significant look. I am on what people might call "the cusp" of normal. I can usually fit into a "L" or "XL" in traditional sizing. But basically, I am fat.

When I was a kid, I was teased for being chubby. My heft wasn't outrageous, and when I look back on photographs of my time in school, I see I wasn't actually fat but significantly bigger than my friends, which was the crime.

Once, when I was in tenth grade and dangerously obsessed with what my boyfriend thought of me, he told me to wear my hair up because it made my face look skinnier. I think I may have taken that advice into my adult life with more than a little intensity.

I am using the word "fat" on purpose. There are other words of course—overweight, big, curvy, chubby, heavy, large, and they all work in this context. But the word "fat" elicits the kind of discomfort and (dare I say) fear that is the driver behind a lot of bias. Fat can be perceived as one of the worst insults you can call a person in our society. Women spend lifetimes trying to avoid the adjective. Some men, too. Fat is an insult; it is almost a dirty word.

I was particularly moved by Aubrey Gordon, who began writing anonymously about the social realities of life as a very fat person, publishing under the name Your Fat Friend. Her 2020 *Medium* piece, "Just Say Fat" implores us to, "Just say 'fat.' Not 'curvy' or 'chubby' or 'chunky' or 'fluffy' or 'more to love' or 'big guy' or 'full-figured' or 'big-boned" or 'queen size' or 'husky' or 'obese' or 'overweight.' Do not rush to correct fat friends who name their own bodies for themselves, using the words that fit their experience. Recognize that a fat person daring to name their own body is an act of growth and that when you correct us, you stunt it. It is also an act of rebellion, and when you silence it, you silence us. Remember that your comfort does not take precedence over our autonomy. Do not rush to soothe and center your own discomfort by insisting, 'Sweetie, no! You're not fat' Let us say our own names for ourselves."[1]

While I was fatter than my friends growing up, I am not and never really have been fat enough where it impacted my life like it has for others. I have friends who live with society's view and disgust of fat people and have been ridiculed and discriminated against their whole lives. I have friends who have lost boyfriends when they gained weight, have been told they were unhealthy and disgusting as a sort of bizarre catcall on the street, and who were told on social media that they should "lay down and die" simply because they were fatter than the norm. All this is much worse than anything I have ever experienced. When I was younger, with some carb cutting, manic exercise, and diet, I could always lose enough weight to be taken seriously. It's different, and I acknowledge that.

It is not easy to be fat in our society, and it is difficult to be fat and in pain. With one look, doctors are often dismissive of health complaints.

According to doctors who use the BMI measurement, those who are overweight have a body mass index (BMI) of 25 or greater, and those who are obese have a BMI of 30 or greater (Note: BMI has received a lot of critique). This means a large number of people going to the doctor for a concern might face unnecessary biases due to their body shape or size.

Dolores, who lives with often debilitating fibromyalgia, recounts her experience with being overlooked because of her weight.

"I can't tell you how frustrating it can be. It took me so many years to really be diagnosed with fibromyalgia, after many doctors appointments. I'm probably forty or forty-five pounds overweight. Doctors told me to come back when I had lost it. When I said I had tried everything, but I couldn't lose even a pound, they looked at me skeptically.

"One doctor said, 'If you don't eat, you don't gain weight. It's easy. Don't eat so much.'

"It's hard not to feel like they must be right. And maybe, on some level they are. But what about right now? I always feel like, 'Okay, but how can you help me right now even if I'm fat?'"

I have had the same experience. Many times I was told my pain would go away if I could just lose twenty pounds. Thirty pounds. I have been handed diet books and then dismissed. I have had my BMI measured to see if I could eke my way into a study of a new weight loss drug (I could but decided against it). I have had (elective) surgery to remove fat around my hips because I believed it would alleviate some of the pain (It didn't.). I have received more than the just direct suggestion that losing weight would be the key to unlocking my pain-free life; the looks and implications were hardest to swallow. There is almost no education on obesity offered in medical school, so it is no surprise that doctors often don't even consider it.

———————

As we look at this from a chronic pain perspective, I think it's worth thinking about how we treat fat people, especially fat women, in our society. While the evidence is there that health-care professionals often dismiss people and their pain because of their weight, there is also an undeniable bias—and dare I say cruelty—directed at those in the world who are considered fat.

This kind of condescension and rejection did not just start when I was an adult in pain. When I was ten, I had a group of friends from school who did not like me very much. In the way we try to please those less eager to accept us, I spent an uncomfortable amount of my days trying to change their minds. I would follow them from the bus stop, tumble into their mudrooms, and listen to their sighs when I settled down on the couch next to them to watch *Three's Company*. Maybe they just thought I was annoying. I was. But a few things lead

me to believe the reason they were so cruel was that I was fat
. . . or fatter than them.

One afternoon after the mudroom, the girls piled into the kitchen to get a snack. One of the leaders wanted to cook bacon, and the others were delighted. Bacon was never my favorite food, but as I usually did, I stayed quiet.

There were only so many chairs at the kitchen table. When I went to sit in one, one of the girls pointed to the floor.

"You can sit there," she said.

Remember, all I wanted was for them to like me, so when they told me to do something, I did it. When the bacon was done, one of the girls tossed it on a paper towel–lined plate and brought the plate to the table. I could see danger in the curl of her smirk.

"Frannie, you want some?" she asked.

I didn't. I shrugged.

And that was when they started snorting. Loud throaty snorts, which could only mean one thing.

"Come on, piggy," they chanted. "Eat that bacon."

They laughed through the chants and snorts so that their faces were red, their eyes crying.

I'll never know if they were calling me a pig and shoving bacon in my face in a really meta way, or if they just forgot pigs *are* bacon, but I didn't care. The shame of this moment has never left me, because, I'm so embarrassed to admit, I *ate* the bacon. And worse, I didn't stand up indignant and march out of the kitchen, the mudroom, the house, and their friend group. I came right back the next day.

I tell this story to paint a picture of where I was coming from when I first went to the doctor about my pain. This was an extreme example, early in my life, but it wasn't the only time I was humiliated because I was fatter than the others. It was so commonplace, I started to expect it. *Oh, he won't want to date me, I'm fat. I shouldn't eat it, even though all my friends are, I should play more sports. I should never wear a bikini. Hide, hide, hide.* It made sense I didn't get into that club or that world. I internalized it so significantly, I took it to be reality. I'm ashamed to say in some ways I still do.

When I started to feel terrible, around my eighteenth birthday, I lost fifteen pounds. I now know I had something off about my thyroid, and my intestines were already rejecting food, but at the time I was thrilled. Friends, counselors, coaches, random adults, even people very close to me (who must have known I was exhausted all the time with puffy eyes and depression) congratulated me on losing weight.

"You look great! You're sexy now."

"What did you do? Tell me so I can do it, too!"

"I always knew you could do it!"

I didn't go to the doctor immediately, and I didn't tell anyone I felt terrible because I was worried they would make me change something and I'd gain the weight back.

Kate experienced this same praise and then happiness to lose weight on medication.

"The anticonvulsant drugs I took for the last two-ish years of my TN had a side effect that affected my blood sugar and metabolism. I knew taking the drugs was making me thinner than I'd ever been. And it was the first time in my life I didn't struggle with my weight or constantly think about weight. I've never admitted this before, but I loved it. It was a fucked-up bonus in my head. I knew, at times, I needed to eat more, and I remember going to an appointment at a pain clinic and meeting a doc for the first time.

"When he left the room, I read his notes. He had written: 'Thirty-year-old female, healthy weight.'

"And my thought was, *This is not a healthy weight for me.* I knew it, and he didn't.

"After my surgery, I had to wean off my skinny drugs. I had blood sugar headaches for weeks. And as I became fuller and my thighs began to return to their larger size, I thought about taking the drugs again, because I may not have pain and may get my life back. *But God forbid I be fat.*"

———————————

I didn't go to the doctor for pain until I was twenty-two. I went because I had a lump on the side of my neck, which was growing. My stomach was rejecting food with alarming consistency, though I wasn't losing any weight. I was swollen. Everything hurt. I could barely stay awake long enough to get to my admin job every morning, and I could almost never stay out past 11:00 p.m. Walking down the subway stairs hurt. Breathing hurt. Opening my eyes hurt.

I went into the endocrinologist afraid. I was afraid I had a lump in my neck, which meant I was going to die. I don't think that was melodramatic. It was the size of a walnut, and it was growing every day.

He asked me to describe how I was feeling.

"I feel so tired all the time, and my muscles hurt when you even graze my leg. And I have this lump." I bent my head back and showed him my neck, though I didn't need to, you could see it when I was upright.

"Ah yes, a nodule. Shouldn't be a problem."

He biopsied the nodule with a needle the length of my forearm.

"Should be fine. You're young," he said.

After the needle had pierced my throat, I struggled to speak.

"How much do you weigh?" he asked afterward, as he entered something in the computer and did not look me in the eye.

"I don't know. 140? 145?"

"And you're how tall?"

"Five feet."

His hands stopped typing. He visibly stiffened. Spinning the chair around he had a very similar smile on his face as my friend in her bacon-full kitchen.

"Well, that's too much," he said. "I think we've found the problem."

"I have a lump on my neck because I weigh too much?" I asked.

"You are seriously overweight, and yes, that has an impact on your health. My guess is this nodule is benign. Maybe a fatty deposit." He laughed at this, though I still don't totally get the joke.

He went on. "I'm sure this is nothing, and when I find out it is nothing, here's what I suggest."

He outlined a 1200-calorie-a-day diet, no carbs, sixty minutes of cardio five times weekly, plus ten glasses of water a day.

"No pain, no gain," he said. "Or, no pain, no loss, actually." He laughed again.

I took the pamphlets he gave me. I couldn't imagine even *walking* for sixty minutes, never mind jogging. One of the only things left in life that didn't make me want to clutch my stomach in agony were carbohydrates. I could stomach a small bowl of pasta with oil or a few pieces of toast without incident. I was barely eating already, and his plan was not going to help.

I have been to countless doctors since who have looked

at me and prescribed diet over further tests. Considering my history, as well as the general disgust our modern society has for fat people, I am particularly sensitive to this reaction. It has felt especially cruel to hear this from doctors because they were supposed to be caring for my health. This kind of language always feels like an attack.

An anesthesiologist once said to me, "Wait, holy moly, is that how much you *actually* weigh?" right before I slid into oblivion.

According to *Impact of Weight Bias and Stigma on Quality of Care and Outcomes for Patients with Obesity*, "Primary care providers and health promotion specialists, who typically demonstrate a commitment to providing care for underserved populations, are unlikely to flagrantly and intentionally discriminate against their patients. Nevertheless, there are several ways that their attitudes about obesity may cause their patients with obesity to feel disrespected, inadequate or unwelcome, thus negatively affecting the encounter quality and their willingness to seek needed care."[2]

In the same study, the authors concluded there was a dangerous cycle of this kind of stigma and subsequent behavior. If a patient was obsese, and the stigma was enacted, the patient felt like they were in a threatening environment. If the environment felt threatening, the patient would be stressed, avoidant of care, have mistrust, have a low probability of adhering to recommendations, and thus use poor communication about their ailments. When all of that was evident, patient outcomes were often negative.

As I talk to other women in pain, and I read of the often-biased treatment of fat women, I understand that sometimes, health-care professionals were not telling me I was fat to diagnose anything aside from general "unhealthiness." They were also, most likely, wrong that my weight was the cause of my suffering.

Here is where I concede it is always better to eat well and exercise to stay healthy. Here's where many people would say being fat *is* being unhealthy, and losing weight is always in anyone's best interest. I don't believe that. I admit there have been times in my life where I ate and drank to excess and those were not good times for my health. But I will not say being fat leads to chronic pain. I have learned it simply isn't true.

I spoke to a lot of women about how people have perceived their bodies during the time they have been in pain. Some of them have had the opposite experience, becoming so skinny people accused them of eating disorders instead of searching for answers. Katie shared her experiences.

"There are a lot of things I have either been told by a doctor to eat or don't eat because they cause my shitty digestive system a great deal of pain. But being a chronically underweight woman with medically necessary food restrictions makes people uncomfortable. Nine times out of ten, they think it's an eating disorder unless I explain the whole thing. If there's any way I can avoid telling people about my dietary restrictions, I will. I don't think I would get as much shit for this if I was a man."

The irony, of course, is there are a lot of factors contributing to body type that no one ever speaks about.

In her piece, *Addressing Weight Bias in Medicine*, Fatima Cody Stanford says, "Obesity is a complex disease that cannot be minimized to the 'calories in/calories out' mantra that has become commonplace. Factors that can contribute to weight might include biological issues such as genetics and hormonal changes that come with aging; developmental issues such as parental obesity; psychological issues including depression or history of trauma; or environmental factors, such as large portion sizes. And these are just a few of a myriad of possible contributors."[3]

Research shows doctors have less respect for patients with higher body mass indexes (BMI), which can alter the care those patients receive.

What do we do about this? While addressing this on a societal level is critical, it will take some time. Already, inclusive sizing and fat celebrity influencers have started to move the dial for cultural change. People like Aubrey Gordon are using their voices for education and activism. That's important and helpful.

But in addition, ". . . Reducing weight stigma in clinical care is a shared responsibility of health-care providers and other clinic staff, as well as the health-care systems/organizations that have the power to implement intervention strategies broadly."

More education is needed for doctors and other health-care professionals about the dangers of attributing pain and disease to obesity. Women in pain have to know their complaints will be taken seriously and not be dismissed if they are overweight. Right now, many of the fat women I interviewed said they would prefer not to go to the doctor at all, save emergency situations. This is clearly not good for their health, their pain, or the health-care system at large.

INTIMACY

Sustaining Relationships in Pain

The sun isn't high yet, and our sheets glow a little bit pink. I wake up slowly these days. Turn over once. Check myself for pain. Turn over twice; check to see if Nick's awake yet. Listen to hear if either of our kids is up. I rub the cat's head. The dog turns over. I scratch her belly.

"Hey," Nick says, his body still hot from sleep. He turns to me and squints into the room. "How are you feeling?" It's a tick, this question.

"I'm okay." It's a lie, this answer.

Nick leans over, across the expanse of bed, and takes my hand. He pulls me toward him. My dark brown hair falls in his eyes, and he brushes it back. I lean in to kiss him, like we have done a thousand million times. His lips brush mine. The tips of our eyelashes touch.

I always assumed I'd be dead by now. That's not hyperbole. For a long time, every time I went to the doctor there was news that could shorten my life. Enough times, and it didn't seem like there was a lot of time left to play with.

I lived for a while like I was sure I would have a thirty-year life. I was narcissistic and entitled and overly romantic. I was pleasure seeking, and I didn't give a lot of thought to the repercussions of my actions or my feelings. Maybe that's the definition of youth. But I can't really blame youth when I think thirty-two is old age.

But I'm still here.

Throughout this whole time, I had a boyfriend who then became my husband and then a father to my children. It's incredible. He stuck with it. And me.

I now know through all of my chronic pain, I was always looking for him to be something he wasn't. Something he could never be. I wanted him to be the *rest of me*—the rest of my future, the rest of my life. Here was my reasoning. If I was going to have half a life then I was half a person and so I looked to everyone else and everything else to make me complete—especially him.

What was most unfair to him, I'm now realizing, was in assuming I'd be dead soon, I was both giving him all of my future and taking all of it away at the same time. What was he supposed to do with the absence of my own belief?

We have come a long way from the beginnings of our relationship . . . from the onset of my pain, from blowups and breakdowns, and from struggles and desperation. We have also come a long way from the blind faith of youth, from inexperience acting as a stand-in for rationale, and from the elation of a relationship with almost no responsibilities but to love each other.

There have been terrible times and wonderful times. I imagine this is true in the undulation of any long-term relationship. But mostly there are the middle times, the times like now. The mornings that glow pink with sunrise. Curled up cats and dogs. Sleeping children. Eyelashes. Even when all of it is shrouded in pain, I'm grateful.

When I was in the depths of pain for one of the first times, before we were even married, Nick bought us cheap tickets to Jamaica. We were twenty-five, and we yearned to outrun the problem, visiting an all-inclusive resort. We'd have nothing to have to think about and nothing we'd have to do. No stress. We'd have beach days, drinks heavy with pineapple, pools, and sun. Soft beds, warm towels, rest. Of course, we weren't outrunning anything, because we brought the pain with us, packed deep in my bones, evident in our every interaction.

The first night we arrived, I sipped a glass of wine and watched the resort show. The stools were bamboo and imprinted a repeating square pattern on my bare legs. I crossed and re-crossed them to get comfortable. It didn't work. Nick stared at the steel drummers, like there was an answer there. I sighed, waiting for enough time to go by that it would be reasonable for me to go up to bed.

Two women walked by, their chests spilling out of bronze bikinis. He may not have meant to, and certainly didn't want me to notice, but Nick's gaze followed them into the beachy night.

One of the women had long red hair and bangs that cut her forehead in two. Her breasts were small but round, and her nipples poked through the thin fabric of her slinky bathing suit. Her friend was heavier, rounder, but strong. Her thighs looked like she biked many miles a weekend. Her bathing suit was sportier than her friend's, but the same color, like they were on a team. The bronze team. They wore nothing but the bikinis, even though it was evening. The restaurant spilled onto the sand, so it didn't seem that inappropriate. They stopped at the bar outside, ordered drinks laden with fruit and ice, and headed out to the edge of the pool, the ocean waves crashing softly behind them.

I looked away before Nick caught me staring at him staring at them. Finally, he looked away as well. He refocused on me but not without effort.

"So this is fun, right?" he asked from behind his tall amber beer.

I could see the reflection of the bikinis in the glass.

"I'm sorry I'm like this," I said. "You deserve someone strong and healthy."

"It's okay," he said. "I'm used to it."

I know how he meant it, but I knew how I meant it, too. I knew he wanted to understand, but I also knew it was impossible for him to.

There was a difference between the pain Nick knew and the pain I had. He had broken bones, sure, and had slight headaches or skin burns. He had cut himself. Had stitches. But acute pain goes away. Even more importantly, we *know* acute pain will go away.

The understanding you have when you stub your toe is that if you wait long enough, the pain will be gone. That sort of psychological understanding doesn't exist with chronic pain. Instead, signals of pain remain active in the nervous system for months or even years. The reality can take both a physical and emotional toll, and it is impossible to explain. The disconnect widens the chasm in our experience. I couldn't understand why he wanted to stay with me. Pity? Responsibility? Love?

I turned to look again at the bronze bikinis. I couldn't help it. They had settled into lounge chairs by the moonlit pool. It was warm enough to swim, and it looked like they planned to, but first they drank. They toasted each other, clinking into the night.

I hated myself for it, but I hated them. They looked so healthy and taut in the blue light of nighttime. They didn't worry their bodies would betray them. They tucked their smooth legs under their tight butts and gossiped about whatever as they guzzled their fruity drinks. They looked like people my boyfriend should be hanging out with. They looked like people my boyfriend should be having sex with. They didn't look like me.

"And anyway," Nick said, "you look great."

He smiled his wide smile and touched my arm. I heard two splashes behind me and imagined the bronze bikinis diving into the heated pool, their slick hair making them only sexier in the steamy night. Nick didn't look. Neither did I. We both wanted to.

Nick was a liar, but he was a loving liar. I looked like absolute shit. I checked myself in the mirror behind the bar. My eyes were rimmed with a yellowish tint. My skin was flaky and beet red from the sun because the medicine I had to take made me sensitive in a new, exposed way. My neck was swollen and my fingernails, for some reason, were blue.

Fuck it, I thought. *I look alien, I feel alien, I need to get back to this earth. I need to get back to my boyfriend. I can't let the bronze team win.* I took a sip of my wine. I felt okay. Encouraged and jealous of the bikinis, I downed it, one long gulp. Just to prove I could.

Nick raised his eyebrows and then raised his glass. "There you go," he said, pleased with me. I could see he thought maybe, just maybe we could have sex later. Maybe just maybe, he could get me back not just as someone to love, but as someone to want.

"Thanks," I said, smiling back at him. And then all of a sudden, maybe because of the mix of medication and alcohol, maybe just from giving in to a moment of saying, "Screw it," and taking a chance, there was a deep pain in my belly, a fire about to explode and I knew I was about to throw up.

With a muttered "I'llberightback," I jumped off the stool and dashed back to our room, three stairways away. I slammed myself through the bamboo bathroom door and didn't make it to the toilet. Orange vomit covered the walls of the bathroom, sliding down the tile in gooey bits. I lay down in the middle of the room on the bath mat, unable to move. A few minutes later, Nick knocked on the door.

"Fran?"

I couldn't answer.

"Fran?" He pushed in the door and took a step back. I'm sure what he saw repulsed him, and though I couldn't possibly move, I imagined retreating even further into myself.

"Oh, honey," he said sadly. He got out a towel and washed the walls with the floral soap from the shower, scrubbing the floor and mopping up the mess.

"I'll be right back," he said, and took the bundle of towels out into the hallway. When he came back in, he had more towels, a pillow, and a glass of water.

"Can you drink this?" he asked gently.

"I don't know if I can sit up."

Nick knelt next to me and slid down onto the mat. He smelled like the floral soap and the saltwater and beer he abandoned. I could only have smelled like vomit. Lifting my head in his hand, he tipped a small sip of water into my chapped lips.

"There," he said.

He put the glass of water down on the floor next to me, and I rested my face on the tile in front of the bath mat, the coolness an astounding relief.

Nick tucked the pillow under my head and covered me with a clean towel.

"You don't have to do this," I croaked.

He ignored me and lay down next to me onto the floor.

"Try to sleep," he said.

His hand traced light circles on my back and right before I drifted off, I thought, *He shouldn't have to do this. I am too much work. He has got to leave me, before it's too late.*

Guilt permeates a relationship like this. He feels guilty when he feels well, or when he can't help me, or when he doesn't want to. I feel guilty when I make him miss things, can't be happy, or push him away. I feel guilty when I'm in pain, which is all the time.

Dependence isn't sexy. Maybe it's intimate, but not in the way you want things to be intimate with your partner in love. The power is all upside down. Without the ability to function on my own, I rely on Nick for too much.

For a while, when things were at their worst, he must have felt more like a nurse than a boyfriend. In his mid-twenties, that had to feel like a sentence.

There have been many times in our relationship when I've wondered why he is still here. I know he loves me. Now we have children together, and I have a better outlook on the future, but before, when I was a pile of limbs on the couch day after day, I assumed he would eventually have had enough.

It gutted me, this knowledge, but it came with an understanding that if he left, he had good reason.

It is so hard to have close relationships when you are in pain. There is always something in the way of intimacy. We always have a piece of our minds devoted to thinking about the pain—how to lessen it, how to avoid more of it, how to live with it—and as that part swells, it obscures the way we interact with everyone else in our lives, especially our partners.

The guilt about this can be crushing. One of the hallmarks of adulthood is the ability to take care of ourselves. When we can't achieve that, when we depend on others to clean up our messes and hold up our heads, we lose our sense of capability, identity, and self. When we become dependent, we are no longer the mature, interesting, sexy adults we want to be. We feel like children or the elderly, and our intimacy, mental health, and understanding of what we deserve suffers greatly for it.

In her piece, "Chronic Pain, Intimacy and Sexuality", Lynn Schlesinger says, "Pain's invisibility has profound implications for social interactions, including sexual relationships."[1]

Of all the subjects I spoke to women about, the one that made them the most upset was how pain has affected their relationships, both with their spouses and their children. It's hard, as a woman who looks relatively healthy most of the time, to exist in the world as a wife, a partner, a mother, and a friend, when we think about pain every minute. We are always fighting against ourselves to put pain aside so we can live up to the expectations we set for ourselves in all of our relationships. Emily shared the following with me:

"I was in a relationship when my joint pain and fainting began.

"It can affect so many aspects (emotional, physical, financial) of a relationship, and neither person will be unscathed. I think it takes a daily commitment to work through those challenges together, and it's something both people need to be on board with. "In my personal experience, our relationship didn't last, and I'd say my illness had a lot to do with it. But it wasn't the only problem in the relationship, so who really knows? I dated here and there, but it's really hard to date when you're mostly confined to your bed. I really just didn't have the energy to date. I was busy keeping myself alive and raising my son."

We have an obligation to our significant others but also to ourselves to be invested in relationships we have committed to. Many of us promise to be there "in sickness and health." But what if the sickness (or the pain) goes on forever? Are the vows that literal?

Intimacy is not only about sex, of course, but because it is so physical, it is often the part of intimacy most difficult to engage in when in pain. Of course, sexuality is critical for connection with our partners and sustainability of our relationships. When we have chronic pain, it introduces a level of complexity that can sometimes be counter to the pleasure supposed to be inherent in sex. It might be about the pain, or the mental illness, or the medication, but often, the idea of being physically intimate with our partners feels fully out of reach.

In a *Practical Pain Management* article, "Improving the Sex Lives of Patients With Chronic Pain," Kristin Della Volpe confirms this. "In surveys of patients with low back pain, for example, nearly 50% of patients reported that pain affects their sexual enjoyment, 72% reported having sex less frequently following the onset of back pain, 70% found their sex life less satisfying after the onset of back pain, and 61% said that their back pain made their relationship with their partner more difficult."[2]

As Schlesinger reminds us, when we are in pain, there are often extra factors standing in the way of intimacy. For instance, "Choosing the 'right time' for being physically intimate [was] is sometimes problematic."[2]

Adele said:

"There was a time many years ago when it became clear I couldn't have sex very much with my husband without it leading to severe pain and exhaustion. It was sad for me, but particularly sad for him, because he felt an enormous sense of rejection around it. I still feel terrible about it all the time."

Because intimacy and pain are both wrapped up in the body, our understanding of "self" can change dramatically when pain is at its most extreme. In her study of twenty-eight women, Schlesinger says, "The impact of chronic pain on sexual experiences depended in part on the women's self-image and sense of worth. In defining pain, some women equated their pain with their 'selves.'"[3]

Of course, there is more to intimacy than sex, and sometimes we can supplement with other kinds of closeness. But even closeness can sometimes be impossible. And when that happens, the connection suffers, and days are shrouded in guilt and regret.

Kate shared with me the following:

"I used to feel so much shame around being the 'broken' wife. I felt guilty Chad and I could not live the daily life we dreamed of because I didn't know what kind of day I would have. There was a time of each year, early on in my journey with TN, where my pain would go into remission. It was always summer. And then, usually in early October, the monster would come roaring back in the shower one day, and I would just crumble into nothing. I would be inconsolable. I was so dependent on my husband and my sister (depending on who was available) in those moments of absolute emotional defeat, and I hated the feeling. I hated being a slave to pain, and I hated the hand of fear that grabbed me in painful moments. My husband did so much protection of me and so much advocating for me, and while it made me love him more, I was afraid it would make him love me less, where I would be a true burden on him."

I heard that word so many times—"burden." When we need help, especially from those who are closest to us, we feel like we are unfairly putting stress and weight onto our relationships. They become uneven and unbalanced. The hardest part, what those vows "in sickness and in health" suggest, is that there will be both, and the ebb and flow of the relationship will be able to sustain itself because there will be back and forth. While a life of chronic pain is not constant "sickness," it never flows into real health. So our partners are forever caregivers, and that's not what either of us signed on for. Jessica told me the following:

"I'm lucky to be married to someone who probably takes it more seriously than I do. He consistently gives me the message that he feels for me and knows it's hard for me. He's always encouraging me to buy new gadgets or try new treatments that might help; and I imagine it helps him when he knows I'm being proactive about it. We joke that the most common gifts he's bought me over the years have been pain-related—and not in a kinky way but much more in a little-old-lady kind of way. I can feel resentful about having to spend my time and our money on things related to my pain, though he thinks there's nothing more important to spend time and money on.

"I do notice in my relationships that I can often try to shield people from my pain. Vulnerability in this area is definitely hard for me, but also, I want to protect people from feeling uncomfortable. I guess I don't want to create a lot of space for my pain in my relationships, and yet it occupies a huge amount of space in my brain."

Leslie also shared her situation.

"It definitely affects my relationships because I really have to keep to a strict schedule and diet to make sure I keep inflammation under control and feel well. I know they [her son and husband] wish I could be more spontaneous or even stay up late on weekends and even drink. When I do make exceptions, I have flare ups, migraines, or can't walk. For me, it's not worth the pain for a night out.

"While family and friends do understand, I've explained it to them many times. I know it would be easier if I could just go with the flow and not have to be difficult. All our vacations have to have an 'evacuation plan' in case I go into anaphylaxis. We can't just book a cruise or a trip without thinking about, 'What if?'"

Of course, not everyone is supportive or kind and sometimes, people who were supposed to love and support us don't follow through. When there is not only a strained connection, but also a real sense of disbelief, the relationship can feel like a constant battle.

Rachel explains,

"I was in a very abusive marriage for fourteen years, and for eleven years prior to my diagnosis, my ex-husband always referred to me as a hypochondriac. He was always saying, 'Oh, there's something new wrong with you every day.' Because I looked normal on the outside, he was treating me like somebody who was just complaining."

It's one thing to struggle with a partner who has seen us at our best and worst but also has a long history and investment in loving us. When it comes to new relationships, things can feel almost impossible. Rachel struggles with how much to tell those she dates.

"I don't share that I have a medical condition immediately with people I'm dating because it can scare people away. Especially when they see me walking around with twenty-five bottles of pills. It can be intimidating and daunting to explain to someone that literally every part of your body is falling apart, and there are a lot of things wrong with you that will never be fixed.

"There is a lot of stigma around medications, especially pain medications. So despite the fact I have many significant conditions tied to one big condition, and many of those are very significantly painful, there's still a stigma surrounding the choice to medicate to take care of it."

What about the relationships that are no longer functioning? How are we supposed to handle already fraught situations when people do not understand us? Emily described her experiences to me.

"I grew up in St. Louis but married and had a child with a man from Indianapolis when I was in college. When I got so sick I was unable to hold down a job, my family in St. Louis urged me to move back home for a time so that we could get me fixed up and back on my feet. My son was nine.

"I reluctantly agreed, but my ex-husband and his wife would not allow me to bring my son over state lines, so I had to make the impossible choice [of my health over seeing my son]. I knew I needed the support of family in order to figure out what was going on and ultimately made the heart-wrenching decision to temporarily move back to St. Louis. I didn't know I'd be put through what I call 'the specialist shuffle.'

"The rheumatologist says, "Hm, I don't know," and sends me to the neurologist.

"He says, 'Hm, not sure what's going on,' who then sends me to the cardiologist.

"He says, 'Yeah, maybe it's just anxiety,' who then sends me on to the psychiatrist.

"He says, 'Hm, maybe it's conversion disorder.'"

"When it's shown it is not, the cycle and shuffle starts all over again. And because it can take months to see a specialist, this is a long, long process.

"What was only supposed to be a few months ended up being four years. And during those four years in St. Louis (I moved back to Indy when my son was thirteen, and then back to St. Louis when he graduated high school), I cashed out my meager savings, my small retirement fund (both of which were depleted in the first year for medical expenses), applied for disability, and became accustomed to living in extreme poverty."

We want to be loved and cared for, but when we are loved and cared for, we feel guilty, and feel like our partners (or family or friends) are doing so out of obligation and pity.

But we are complicit in creating and sustaining that narrative. Maybe those emotions we suppose they *must* feel are actually not there at all, or maybe if they are there, they are a miniscule part of a much bigger picture. Certainly, this isn't always true, and there are situations in which our interpretation of the situation is correct. But we can only learn the truth if we ask. Our job is to tell the stories of our reality clearly and completely. Then we have to ask our partners and loved ones whether that reality is too much. If they feel they can't handle it, wouldn't it be better for us both to know?

We think our narrative is ours alone. If we keep quiet and ashamed, I suppose it's true. But I now can understand it is possible and necessary to include other people in our narrative, especially those who love us. We can let their experience be part of the story, too.

MOTHERHOOD

Raising Children While in Pain

My daughter locked herself in the house one day. She was about eighteen months old. Her older brother was in preschool, but she wasn't old enough yet, so we had a babysitter, we'll call her Sandra, with her during the day while I was in graduate school.

Sandra went outside to get something from the stroller. When she tried the door to get back into the house, it was locked.

She called me, frantic.

"She's in there, and I'm out here, and I don't know what to do."

I was fifteen minutes away, kicking myself. It seemed in those days I was always fifteen minutes away and kicking myself.

"Isn't there a key in the hidden turtle?"

"I looked. It's not there."

"Call the police, I'll be right there."

I rushed to the car, sped home, and arrived in less than fifteen minutes.

When I got to the house, the babysitter, on the roof of the mudroom, stared at my baby through the window to her nursery. Sandra was balanced on her knees, leaning forward. It was fall and chilly, and she was only wearing a tank top and jeans. She was making funny faces at my daughter, and my child was up against the window, her little nose smooshed flat against the glass, laughing and playing along. She was not scared at all. I grabbed at my side to find my purse where I kept the house key. I did not keep it with my car keys because I hate a bulky key ring flopping around. We rarely had to unlock the doors—one of us or the babysitter was always home—so I rarely used it. I kept it secure in the inside pocket of my purse, zipped.

My purse was not at my side. I ran to the car. It was not on the passenger seat where it should have been. I racked my brain, trying to remember why I would have my car key but not my purse, especially in a situation in which I needed my house key. Then it hit me. I had left too fast. I had put my car key in my jacket pocket and sprinted to the car. And I had left my purse on my desk, fifteen minutes away.

A ladder leaned against the house. I found out later that instead of calling the police right away, Sandra had yelled over the fence to a neighbor, and he had rushed over with his ladder.

"Holy shit. I don't have my key. I can't believe this. I left it on my desk." My breath became shallower. "Are you okay? Is she okay? Did you call the police?"

"Yes, the police are coming. I called them. I just didn't want her all alone. The key wasn't in the turtle, and your neighbor was so helpful. I was hoping the window would be open, but it's locked." She was calm. How was she so calm when my child was a pane of glass away? "He ran home. He's getting something to open the window, if the police don't come soon."

My neighbor rushed into the yard, breathing heavily, holding a crowbar.

"She okay?" he called.

Sandra nodded.

"No key?" he asked.

I shook my head.

"Should I go up there, or are you going to go up?" He looked at me, the crowbar outstretched.

I stood taking in the scenario, but I did not move. I knew the second I tried to climb the ladder one of two things was going to happen. Either my back would give out halfway up from the effort of climbing and I'd fall backward onto the decking, or I'd get to the top by some miracle, sit in front of the window, trade places with Sandra, and then not be able to get up again.

In those days my back went out with almost no cause. I'd be walking down the street and all of a sudden I'd be clutching a parking meter, inching my way down to the curb. I'd be in a yoga class that I took to try to help my joints, and I'd get stuck in Child's Pose, asking the teacher for a hand getting up to limp to the locker room.

If I climbed the ladder, I'd either seize up and fall off of it, or, if the adrenaline kicked in, I'd get to the roof and eventually seize up there. In either case, someone would have to save me, and I was not the one who needed saving.

The police arrived as I was trying to figure out what I should do. Sandra stayed on the roof until the police got the door open, and then I rushed in.

I went up the stairs as fast as I could (which, because of my back, was not that fast) and I dove onto my daughter's shag rug, scooping her into my arms, my back tightening like it was in a vice. But it was okay because I wasn't on the roof. I was on a rug, and I knew I could lie there and eventually the spasm would cease, and I could be somewhat useful again. My daughter thought it was fantastic that I had collapsed onto the rug to play with her. She hugged me and then pointed to her pile of stuffed animals, wanting to play. I surveyed the room, all of the potential dangers she could have gotten into, and then I looked at the windowpane. Sandra still sat on the shingles, hand up against the glass. She smiled, got up, and made her way back down the ladder, meeting us back inside and helping me up onto a chair.

The police left, and Nick was traveling, so it became clear pretty quickly that the rest of the day was going to be a challenge. If I wanted to be able to stand, I'd have to take a muscle relaxer, which made driving impossibly dangerous, and I wouldn't be able to pick up my son. If I didn't take the pill, I'd be sitting crooked on a chair for the rest of the night, unable to walk, and not able to take care of two toddlers.

"I'll stay. I can get him from school," Sandra said.

She didn't even have to ask me if I'd be okay. She knew, because she had been with us a long time already, that I wouldn't.

"You don't have to," I whispered. We both knew that was a lie.

Sandra picked up my son, prepared dinner, bathed my daughter, and helped me to bed. I sank deeper into myself at the realization that had I been alone, I would have done everything possible to get on the roof and then take care of my children. But I also knew how difficult it would have been, and I might not have made it. My child would have been in a house of cleaning solution poison, knives, sockets, and stairs, and I would have been helpless. If Sandra wasn't there, I would have called someone to help me, maybe my already heroic neighbor. Whether it was the babysitter or my neighbor or a friend or my family, I would have had to call someone to help me. I called people to help me all the time. I needed help with everything physical about having children, and it crushed me. The guilt of this truth seeped into the already deep well of anxiety gouged into my chest until it overflowed.

My baby was fine. Sandra was fine.

She remains a heroine to me for this and many smaller heroic feats. Like all children, both of mine have endured and been fine in hundreds of situations after this. Some I could and some I could not handle.

But it was hard, when I saw a healthy, able person saving my child, to not feel like I owed my kids more than I could give them. I felt selfish in wanting them, and wondered if I made the wrong choice. When I had children, something shifted. I'll admit it was small. It took me a very long time to pivot enough that I could see something real in front of me. It was years before I believed in a future. The first few years of being a mother convinced me I was not going to make it. It was so physically difficult for me, I wasn't sure I'd be able to get through.

When a baby screamed in the middle of the night and I turned over to get up—a starburst of pain shot from my hip. When I ate something "off," I had to nurse on the toilet. When I rocked in the chair, I had to keep my neck completely still or I'd cry more than the infant. When I lifted my toddlers, my back went out. I once spent seven hours on the floor with my two-year-old, not because I was a devoted mother and wanted to play but because there was absolutely no way I could get up. In the first few years of my children's life, my pain ballooned into its own amoeba, competing for attention in every situation, driving me, not so slowly, mad.

I spoke to other mothers with chronic pain, and I was not alone in feeling like this. Mothers in pain are racked with guilt and feelings of inadequacy. It is hard not to assume our children will be worse off with us than if they had pain-free mothers.

For many of us, we ignored the potential for disaster when it came to having children, because it was something we always knew we wanted to do. Some of us were lucky enough to be able to push through the pain.

Jessica said:

"I always knew I wanted to have kids, and I never considered letting back pain stop me. I was concerned about how pregnancy and having babies was going to impact my pain level. But actually my back felt really good when I was pregnant with both of my kids, and when they were babies I remember just sort of muscling through it— there was no way around it; it was what it was, I didn't have a lot of time to focus on my own needs."

Some of us couldn't ignore the reality having children would ignite. Before she had the surgery that tempered her pain, Kate was flattened by the idea of having children.

"I would not have been able to have kids with TN. I know there are people who do, and those are super-human beings. I never could have been even half the parent I wanted to be, living with TN. I also don't know if I physically could have survived labor and delivery with TN. It was my biggest question while I had TN, and the subject of children would just make me stop breathing. I was supposed to be a mother. I had to be a mother. But I could not be a mother with this monster."

Ultimately the surgery she had made her everyday life possible and put having children back on the table.
She says,

"I remember, a month or so after my surgery, walking in the park with my husband and talking about our future children and actually believing it was possible. I could breathe again."

Of course not everyone can do it, even if they want to. Adele choked up a little when I asked her about motherhood.

"In my mind, I always wanted children. I come from a big family, and there are always little kids running around. But once it became clear it was going to be difficult to have them, we stopped trying. It was too hard to imagine even more uncertainty and pain in my life, and when I really stopped and looked at it, I didn't believe having a baby was the right decision. I'm still sad about it."

It is physically and emotionally draining to care for children when we are in pain, even more so when our children have limitations and may be in pain themselves.
Rachel explained her condition to me.

"My condition is very frustrating, and as a parent of a disabled and medically fragile child, I have to push through even when I don't want to. This can leave me with anxiety and depression. It sometimes feels very overwhelming and sad when I come face-to-face with the fact that I will have this for the rest of my life. It will get worse, when I can't remember a time where I wasn't in pain. It is also hard when I'm in chronic pain all the time. It can leave me short-tempered and easily angered. Oftentimes people in chronic pain don't sleep well. When I finally got my diagnosis, I felt really vindicated and I thought that it would change things. Unfortunately it did not.

"Children are children and they only think about children's things. So even though mine might understand I'm in pain, they're still going to be disappointed if I can't take a four-hour hike with them."

The *Journal of Nursing Scholarship* published a study in 2013 entitled, "The Shroud: The Ways Adolescents Manage Living With Parental Chronic Pain." The researchers interviewed thirty adolescents who grew up with parents who lived with chronic pain.

What they found confirms our worst fears as mothers. Children who have parents "shrouded" in pain are at a serious disadvantage. They were found to "endure hardships; distance themselves; lament losses; and hold back on revealing their authentic selves."[1]

In her 2014 *Atlantic* piece, "Parenting Through Chronic Physical Pain," Rachel Rabkin Peachman analyzes a myriad of studies of children with parents in pain.

As a pain sufferer herself, her interpretations are as chilling as the data. In reviewing "The Shroud," she states, "The researchers interviewed a group of 30 adolescents who grew up with parents experiencing chronic pain. In many cases, the children felt their parents were uninvolved physically and/or emotionally, and more likely to be irritable, hostile, and unpredictable. Because of this, the children often hid their true feelings and needs from their parents, lived in fear of stressing their parents out or causing their parents pain, took on a caretaking role before they were ready to do so, and questioned whether they were to blame for their parents' suffering. The children and young adults dealt with these feelings in various ways—becoming perfectionists, retreating in silence, or turning to substance abuse. Reading these outcomes broke my heart."

She goes on, "In *The Journal of Pain*, a 2006 study is particularly discouraging. The study compared 39 mothers with chronic pain to 35 mothers who were not in pain. The mothers with chronic pain reported that they were more likely to be lax in their parenting and that the quality of their relationships with their children suffered compared to mothers without pain."[2][3]

In addition, in a 2012 study, "Chronic Pain in Parents Appears Associated with Chronic Pain in Adolescents, Young Adults", the researchers concluded that "both maternal chronic pain and paternal chronic pain are associated with chronic nonspecific pain and especially with chronic multisite pain in adolescents and young adults. Moreover, we found a substantial increase in pain among offspring for whom both parents reported chronic pain."[4]

It doesn't look great. Does this mean that we are right to live in a constant state of guilt and worry about what will happen to our children? Maybe. But I'm not willing to throw in that particular towel. When I read these outcomes, and stew in my own guilt, I have to wonder if there is any way we could look at this from a different angle. Could I possibly pivot to thinking that having a mother with chronic pain might help my children in life? Might it give them empathy they otherwise would not have?

I'm not alone in thinking this. In her piece, "Parenting with Chronic Pain," Sarah Erdreich states, "In my more optimistic moments, I think of the possible upsides. I hope that having a disabled mother will give my daughter an object lesson in empathy and patience, and increase her comfort around people with different capabilities. I hope that having a father who takes on the bulk of domestic duties and parenthood responsibilities will show her how fluid gender roles can and should be. And I hope that she'll see that having a disability doesn't mean that specific limitations are the sum total of a person's life."[5]

We have to hope that's true. Faced with all the research, it's hard to do. But what choice do we have? Like any adversity in life, living with a parent in pain has to be seen as a way for our children to build resilience, one of the hallmarks of successful adulthood. Sure, we can't always be the upbeat, energetic parents we once hoped we would be, but we can do other things, smaller things, which connect us to our kids in important ways. Maybe we can even simply be around more, since we move more slowly and deliberately . . . to be, as Emily said below, "a soft place to land."

"Sure, there are *a million* things I wish I could've done with my son. I wish I could have taken him to more places, given him more cultural experiences, and hiked and biked great trails. But financial and physical limitations were something I couldn't change, so we adapted. In his teenage years, we got into documentaries and had great conversations about them. I taught him how to drive, albeit in short spurts. I was able to be a supportive, soft place to land when he struggled in school. I taught him how to use public transportation when we didn't have a car for five years. I taught him empathy and kindness toward strangers. I hope I've been able to give him things money can't buy because we had to learn as we went along."

Like I worried about my future with my husband, I worried about having children. Instead of offering myself as their selfless mother, I would be asking them to fill me up as my children . . . to complete me. In having children, I reasoned, I was building a future I wasn't expecting. Not existing as a full participant in their childhoods would clearly be unfair to them, and unfair to Nick and to me. I fought this argument with myself for a long time.

I don't know if I ever resolved it. But each year that goes by I am less terrified by the prospect of a truncated future. Each moment that goes by I am humbled by my children's existence and what it has done to my present.

In my quest to be someone they can rely on and be proud of, I have cut out almost everything I used to do that put stress on my body, including work outside my house, most social engagements, fried and processed food, unnecessary conflict, intense physical effort, and difficult relationships, in order to do the everyday job of raising them. I refuse to let my pain make me into a mother I abhor, but the refusal takes a lot of work. I don't always succeed. I think this battle will be one I fight forever. But I'm willing to believe in forever, which is new to me.

Emily came to a similar conclusion.

"At a certain point, my body couldn't keep up. Who knows when the auto-immune issues started, but the symptoms made themselves clear when I was nearing thirty years old. My son was nine at the time. He was into basketball, but I couldn't shoot hoops with him anymore. I adapted—I sat on the sidelines and cheered him on. We swam in the summer because I felt weightless in the water (being in water—even in a bath—is often the only time my joint pain lessens), and we baked cookies in the winter. But we didn't bake from scratch—too much energy and too much standing. The first time I fainted was in the kitchen, in front of him, and I never wanted him to experience that again. We got box mixes and sometimes added our own little flair—a little honey here, some M&M's there—because it was the time we spent together that counted."

Something big happens when you have children and it's not as straightforward as you think.

I used to think when I had children, the world would open up, and I would see it from a wider perspective. I thought I'd meet more people, have more adventure, do more activities, play more.

But what I now know is that the opposite happens. The world closes in. Every choice I make is made with the recognition that it affects a relatively helpless creature immeasurably. Everything I *don't do* is so much more important than anything I do. And it seems like everyone is watching. Maybe this isn't true. Maybe no one cares in the way it feels like they care when I'm no longer the protagonist in my own life.

Every time I couldn't lift my kid, or my back went out, or my head spun, or I wanted to stay in bed all day, I heard in my mind, *Lazylazylazylazy, selfishselfishselfishselfish, badmotherbadmotherbadmother*. My world collapsed in on itself. Gravity pushed me to the ground, and I couldn't move. I broke my own heart.

But things change. Life unfolds, creased and worn. It has gotten physically easier to be a mother. Eventually their incessant physical needs waned.

One day I woke up, and he didn't call me to change him. She didn't ask me to lift her up when she was afraid. He was able to bathe himself, though he still liked me to sit on the lid of the toilet and sing songs with him into the steamy room. She was able to make herself a bagel even though she was too slow with the cream cheese and the heat of toasting made it slip off in lumps.

I was thirty-five, then forty, then forty-four. They were four and six, then eight and ten, then ten and twelve. My end was not in sight. I was still alive. I was in pain every moment of my waking hours, and even some when I was not awake. But I was still here, which had to mean something. I had to mean something. I had to start living.

Living is hard. Having children is hard. But one thing we learn as humans is that two things can be true at the same time. We can be in pain and also happy. We can *not* be able to do things with our children that we want to do but still have meaningful moments and relationships with them. We can fail and still love. We can do the very best we can, and it can be enough.

WELLNESS

In Pursuit of Our Best Selves

When I was in my early thirties, I went to a three-day retreat in Northern California. It was beautiful there, the rocky coastline and rosy-cheek chill a perfect backdrop for a weekend devoted to health and wellness. It was part writing, part wellness, heavy on the wellness. The retreat description was vague, but the overall message on the website seemed to be aimed at people like me—creatives currently lost in a sea of pain or general feelings of being "unwell." It promised an opportunity to address my pain from a place outside of traditional Western medicine, using writing, movement, sound, and nutrition to reset my body.

The retreat was significantly more expensive than I could afford. I did it anyway. My reasoning, as with my reasoning for all treatments/experiences I have tried over the last twenty plus years, was that if it worked, I could cut everything else out. I would not have to spend so much money chasing after a lasting and potent remedy; I would finally have health.

The wellness industry is not new. While companies like Goop and Lulu Lemon have certainly changed the conversation to one of equating money and health, the idea of "wellness" was conceived in the 1950s by Dr. Halbert L. Dunn. He was the first to draw a distinction between *health* and *wellness*.

Health is the absence of sickness. Wellness is something we should be striving toward indefinitely. It is currently a 3.7 trillion-dollar industry and always growing, maybe because you can never really achieve it.[1]

What this says to me is that the goal of wellness should be an ongoing pursuit. It is our personal, singular job to control and steer toward it, and if we remain sick or in pain, we have failed.

I certainly received that message at the retreat. I arrived at the center on a Friday. The website suggested participants arrive with ample time to take in the scenery, walk around the campus, meditate, or settle in whatever way we chose. Back then, I moved at the pace of a geriatic turtle, so the idea of settling into the space was welcome.

I dropped my things in a room I would be sharing with two other women (something extremely nerve-racking for anyone suffering from an explosive stomach disease). I had requested a private room but was told sharing space with others on the same journey would help me with my own.

I started down the path toward the yoga hut, an octagonal room in the middle of the forest with a wood-burning fireplace in the center. It sent up plumes of clove-scented smoke into the surrounding air. I was immediately calmed and intrigued.

I knew the retreat hadn't officially started yet, but I poked my head in the door and was surprised to see a young woman sitting near the stove in meditation. She sat in a lotus position, eyes closed, fingers perched on her knees, a tiny smile curving her lips.

I backed out slowly, not wanting to interrupt.

"You can join me, if you like," she said, keeping her eyes closed.

I was at a juncture in my life in which I had decided to say "yes" to things after years of having to say "no." My stomach was somewhat stable, my joints, while stiff and achy, were not on fire, and my brain functioned decently. I was in pain but not immobile.

"Sure." I sat down a few feet from her, smelling her sweat mix with the earthy scent of the fire. She was young, maybe even younger than me. Blond curls balanced on the top of her head like a crown. Her skin glowed. She oozed health, like if she opened her mouth, purified air would come out.

"Do you meditate?" she asked.

"No."

"We'll teach you."

If it hadn't been clear already, it was now. She was one of the facilitators I'd be spending the weekend learning from.

"I'm Desdemona," she said.

I was taken aback because I remembered a bio on the website, which mentioned an Ashley who looked kind of like her, though maybe with brown hair. I did not remember a Desdemona, which should have been my first clue that she was probably a fraud.

"Francesca."

"Welcome, Francesca. I have to tell you, your energy is rancid."

Attempting to be open, I tried to ignore the harsh word.

"Rancid?" I asked.

"I don't mean to be cruel, but that's why you're here, right? To rid yourself of whatever rancid stuff is inside?"

"I'm in pain, and I'd like to be in less pain, if that's what you mean."

During this entire exchange, she kept her eyes closed.

"That's sort of what I mean. But the pain is from other kinds of pain, no?"

"What do you mean?"

I was feeling like this impromptu therapy session was odd and somewhat dangerous. I backed up but felt as though she could sense me leaving through her eyelids.

"Trauma." She fluttered her eyes but they did not open. "We all have childhood trauma. We have a responsibility to our inner child to get it out."

I had thought I was coming to a weekend of writing, Downward Dogs, and kale, possibly some mantra work to trick my mind into thinking I was in less pain. I had not signed up for fireside therapy, particularly from a woman who couldn't be bothered to look at me.

"I'm just gonna . . . go back . . ."

She smiled bigger. "You can resist it, and that's okay. I hope by the end of the weekend, you will hear what I have to say."

I nodded, though she couldn't see it, and beelined it out of the yoga hut, tripping slightly on the threshold.

When I got back to the dorms, I met my roommates, both nice, seemingly normal women, who had experienced pain in some way for their whole adult lives.

"I just need a reset," one of them said.

"I'm excited for the fresh fruit," the other one responded.

In the evening, we had dinner in a mess hall with long tables, long benches, and glowing people at the heads. Everyone up there looked stretched out, like they were made of taffy.

Desdemona sat there with three people I assumed were our other teachers. They laughed a lot but didn't address us. It felt more like a middle school cafeteria than it did a healing circle.

The next day we took a sunrise yoga class. Marc, the teacher, spoke about daily attention to wellness as a key to our overall health, and attributed his own banishment of pain to the hours he spent practicing yoga and eating vegan. This teacher was more grounded and calm than my smiling therapist from the evening before, and I settled in with relief. Until Desdemona sat down on the mat next to me.

"I have decided you will be my special project," she said.

"Not sure I agree to that," I said under my breath, but she didn't hear me.

The class continued, my self-proclaimed mentor outshining everyone in the class with perfect headstands, effortless pigeons, endless tree balance, and glowing arms.

When we were finished, I tried to sneak away, calling to my new friends in an effort to get rid of her, or at least make it clear I wasn't down for this.

She caught up, tucked her sweaty arm through mine, and began a steady stream of words, which didn't cease for the whole weekend.

"Forget the medication and the complaining. Forgive yourself. Manifest what you need. The universe will provide it. Anything. You put rancid energy in the air, that's what you'll get back. Eat well, meditate, exercise. That's all you need."

Taking care of body and mind is a good thing. Plenty of people have improved their overall health because they have focused on what the wellness industry offers. Since this weekend, I have been to countless yoga classes, hundreds of therapy appointments, and even some other retreats. Many of them helped. Many of the tools and habits I learned in these settings have been beneficial to me and my body.

Never have I felt as vividly broken as I did with Desdemona during that weekend. Never have I felt so blamed.

When we try the drugs and they fail, or we refuse them because of potential horrific side effects or because there is not enough research behind them, we sometimes try to take healing into our own hands. We turn to alternative medicine, herbs, yoga, and holistic practitioners of all kinds. We fight. We believe. And sometimes we make a dent in our pain. But sometimes the yearning to be well clouds the basic fact that this general idea of wellness and mindfulness will not stop the pain we live with. Failing at wellness is its own kind of defeat. This failure can lead to a deep and absolute surrender.

Samantha articulated this.

"My first thought about the word 'wellness' is tired and overused. I really do think some things I've tried to manage my pain—really, manage my life—have helped. I'm thinking specifically of acupuncture and massage. I've also done healing meditations through different yoga classes over the years that I do believe helped because they fostered deep relaxation. But honestly, I find that the promises of so many are overstated. Many things offer temporary relief. Nothing is a long-term cure."

Throughout the three days I was at the retreat, Desdemona didn't leave my side. Even when I tried to sneak into my room at the end of the night, she would be at the door, chanting some inspirational mantra into my ear. My roommates commiserated with me about her, but I think they were just glad they didn't have to deal with her.

I didn't stop taking my medication. I started to do yoga, and I ate better for a time, but I knew what Desdamona said was not wholly true. She believed it, though. She must have had some sort of exorcism of rancidity, which helped her in her past. I don't think she was trying to hurt me. But it occurred to me then, and I am certain now, if she had gotten her way, I'd have gotten much sicker, and I'm sure there were people who did.

Dr. Tom Curran, assistant professor in the department of psychological and behavioral science at London School of Economics and the British Psychological Society, articulates that which I feel innately.

"[W]hen you put pressure on people to better themselves and don't talk about the things around them that they can't control, that leads to a lot of self-blame and a lot of self-criticism."[2]

You can argue that you can control your body and pain. I would argue that you are wrong. Certainly, to an extent, particularly when you are starting from a place of health and no pain, you can do things to maintain a sense of control. But all it takes is one moment—one slip, one test result, one twinge—and it becomes clear you never had control at all. Which is why I find the culture of wellness so dangerous. Working out, eating well, meditating, taking supplements, and easing stress in work and relationships are all good things. But you can do all of them and still have horrible pain. It is not your fault.

Sheree had a similar experience with wellness. She went to a workout class at the gym, which professed intensely that wellness was all someone needed. She felt it was almost a cult.

"I would go in, the lights would be low, the music quiet but pulsing. The teacher would tell everyone his personal story of how to live life in a state of wellness—he told the exact same story every week to almost the same set of people—and they ate it up. I admit he was very healthy looking. He looked like whatever he was doing, he was doing something right."

I asked her what she thought about how he presented health and wellness and if it worried her.

"It was just that everyone in that room, men and women, but many more women, wanted to be just like him. He would tell them about a seed he was eating, a fast he was doing, a vitamin, a kind of water, and the next day the whole class was singing its praises. It wasn't really his fault, but the pull of the healthy body and mind was so strong, it was like people couldn't resist."

I asked her how she felt, as someone with chronic pain, when he promised this kind of healing.

"At first I fell for it hook, line and sinker. I bought the seeds. I took the vitamins. I attended class every single day. But I never felt better. Months I did this. Eventually I felt duped, but not as badly as I worried for everyone else. By then I knew he couldn't save me, these people were desperate for it."

When I suggested maybe the other participants in the class did not suffer pain in the way Sheree does, she responded,

"Maybe that's true, but I knew some of those folks. They were ornery New Yorkers. They complained. They worried. They were not gullible, not usually. It was the certainty, the absolute promise I didn't like. I'm all for positivity. This was something else."

I think Sheree's teacher was offering hope. As I have said, I have no problem with hope. I think a lot of wellness is not snake oil, and there are a lot of things in our everyday lives we can change to be healthier and treat our bodies better, which might address some of our pain. But I do not believe in the idea we can save ourselves through wellness, or we can get healthy enough to exorcise our pain. It's dangerous because what happens when we can't? Have we done the yoga wrong? Have we not fasted long enough? Are we holding onto trauma we could let go of? Again, is the problem we are facing because we aren't trying hard enough? Will we never be our best selves? Is it all our fault?

Wellness, as an offering, can feel weak up against a life of severe pain. Everything helps a little. Nothing helps enough.

Candace agreed with me.

> "I have stubbornly refused to just fucking do yoga, no matter how many times it's recommended . . . I found a chiropractor helpful, but haven't done it much since it's rarely covered by insurance. I've done acupuncture for the migraines (it helped, but not for long enough). I once tried the Whole 30 program. I did feel good during those thirty days, but such a restrictive diet is just not long-term tenable for me. I like food. I also took magnesium infusions for a little while; like the acupuncture, they helped, but the effect wasn't long-lasting. God bless every physical therapist and professional masseuse who has given me a deep tissue massage, though."

It can be maddening that many of us *are* open and eager for the wellness solutions offered to us to be the magic break we yearn for. Many of us will try anything (and even try it more than once) to get the results we are promised. Often, the wellness strategy works. It just never works enough.

Jessica shared her thoughts on wellness with me.

> "My first thought when I hear the word 'wellness' depends on my mood, honestly. I wish I could say my reaction is

always, 'Yes. Control what I can. Be proactive and do what I can, in all areas, to help myself. Every little bit helps.' So while that is sometimes my reaction, at other times my first thought is, 'Yeah right. I've tried so many things, and nothing helps enough.' I try to allow myself those times of frustration and hopelessness, too—it's all part of it—and then when I can, I try to just bring myself back to doing what I can for myself.

"In terms of wellness solutions, I've tried to be open to anything, and I do believe in the importance of a focus on wellness strategies for management of chronic pain. I've tried yoga, acupuncture, chiropractic work, muscular activation technique, massage therapy, and probably others. Being proactive about my pain feels good, and I like and believe in the idea of doing what I can. It's just that I don't always have the energy for it, it all takes dedication and time and money, and sometimes that is overwhelming. I get tired of the emotional roller coaster, and I've come to accept (mostly) that 'wellness solutions' are less 'solutions' and more 'management strategies.' I can say that almost all the treatments I've tried have felt like they have helped a little, in the short term, and I try to have that be enough.But I tend to go in and out of treatments over time depending on mood, motivation, energy, space in my life, etc."

Of course, wellness can reap benefits as easily as it can cause harm. Sometimes those two things can happen at the same time.

Leslie explained to me the following:

"Wellness to me is a big umbrella that encompasses so many different parts of mind, body, and soul. I know when I don't sleep or eat well, my body is inflamed, and everything feels off. I can't think or focus, and emotionally it's harder to process things. After years of pain, I have tried everything between yoga, infrared sauna, cryotherapy, salt floats, meditation, chiropractic services, diets, physical therapy, etc. While some have helped a little, others have caused more pain and damage.

"I have learned the difference between good pain and bad pain and know when to stop and take care of myself. I have talked to professionals who have said, 'Try whatever you think will help.' "Meditation, nutrition, and exercise have helped the most. Meditation has allowed me to get out of my head, calm my thoughts, and relax my body. I notice a big difference when I make good nutritional choices for my body. I don't have any food allergies, but my body has big autoimmune reactions to certain types of foods. For someone who struggles with an eating disorder, any food restrictions cause additional anxiety and physical reactions. Knowing how important it is to my wellness makes decisions easier.

"Exercise is also very important for me and has evolved over the years. My body no longer needs or wants long and hard workouts. I focus on moving every day and doing short, mindful exercises and activities. This combination has helped keep my physical and emotional well-being grounded and happy. I wear a bracelet that says, 'Self-care is not selfish.' I am learning to listen to my body and recognize what it needs to feel well."

I think, in the end, that's all any of us is trying to do—listen to our bodies and recognize what they need. Sometimes it is a long walk. Sometimes it's a bowl of kale with lemon. Sometimes it's acupuncture, or cryotherapy, or magnesium, or yoga retreats. Sometimes it's a vat of French fries. A long conversation. No conversation. Sometimes it's binging TV. Sometimes it's sleep or water or pain medication. Sometimes it's nothing—sometimes doing absolutely nothing to alleviate pain is exactly what our bodies are telling us to do. And while I do admit that doing nothing is easier than doing something, I stand by the idea that trying to fix yourself will always be a losing battle. You can heal, of course. You can live a life with less pain than you had yesterday. In terms of wellness, the question is: At what cost?

KINDNESS

A Root of Healing

I have been a little harsh on medical professionals and other health and wellness practitioners in this book. I have experienced—and the women I interviewed have also experienced—repeated dismissal, silencing, and shame by some of the people who were supposed to care for us. But these are not the only experiences I have had, and many people in my pain-related life have been saviors. I have had many doctors, nurses, aids, therapists, instructors, and friends who have done everything in their power to make me well. My gratitude runs deep.

I want to spend some time on kindness. I have hinted at how wonderful my family—particularly my husband—and my friends have been over the years. I have been insanely lucky to be surrounded by so much care and love. Hopefully, I have expressed my gratitude frequently and sufficiently enough that they know how important it has been in my life. If I haven't (or even if I have), I'll try harder to make sure they know it. This book isn't the place to chronicle all of the small and big ways the people closest to me have loved me because it would get us too off track. But I wanted to make sure I spoke about (and let other women speak about) the kindness that emerges when in pain, sometimes from the most unlikely places.

Earlier, I recounted the story of the woman in the black staff T-shirt at the gym who helped me wash my clothes when they were caked in feces. I will never forget her because it would have been so easy for her to ignore me, screw up her face, and sprint away. But she didn't. She looked at me covered in shit and humiliation, and she didn't just smile, she didn't just say something sweet. She reached out her hand and asked to help, which is angel-level work. In that moment, I wasn't as outwardly grateful as I should have been.

Shame can cloud even the most beautiful human offering. But I think about it, and her, all the time, and I hope she knows how important the moment was to me.

When I think back on my twenty-plus years living in pain, moments like that are more frequent than I expected.

Sometimes, the muck of pain leaves us feeling like there's no goodness out there, that no one can understand and therefore no one can care. But that's not true.

When I was nineteen, I was bedridden for what would be the first of many times. I wasn't in huge pain then, but when I looked at the trajectory, it was probably when things started to go really badly. It was scary. I was so tired, getting out of bed seemed impossible. It was only my second year of college in California, where the people I was close to didn't know me too well. I disappeared for a time, and I remember thinking, *I can lie here forever, and it's possible no one will miss me.*

I lived in a room the size of two twin beds, but my roommate had a boyfriend and lived with him in that way most people do when newly in love. I had a little extra room to maneuver, but it also meant I was alone a lot. I had friends, but it was all new, and one year of outdoor-circle civics lectures and beer pong tournaments (for them, not me) didn't make for intensely close relationships with even the "best" of my friends.

I had an RA, we'll call him Adam, the year before who I had bonded with. We were both Jewish and from different parts of the country where Jewish people lived, and there weren't a lot of people I felt so similar to in California. It felt familiar. I had never really looked at the word "familiar" as being derived from the word "family," but once I moved to the other side of the country, it was clear to me that things you feel like you know can stand in pretty seamlessly for things you know.

Adam and I got fairly close. He was dorky and funny, like the boys of my youth, and he behaved the way I expected people to behave, which was much different from the way they did in California. But by the time of my immobility, he was gone, having graduated and moved on to adulthood. Coincidentally, he came back to campus on the second weekend of my bed prison. I don't remember him telling me he was coming, and I can't imagine it had anything to do with me.

But when he got to campus, he called me. I figured he called to tell me he was in town and to come by the football stadium to say hi. But when he called, I didn't answer. He called again. And I didn't answer again. By the third time he called me and I didn't answer, he called my roommate to ask where I was. And she didn't know. (I should mention that she was, and is still, one of my best friends, and she was just away for a long weekend.)

Adam left a college football game to make sure I was okay. It was a big deal because the years before, he had been the mascot. In our college this was a very big thing. He was essentially a celebrity and coming back to school to go to a football game was his version of a reunion tour.

He knocked on the door about twenty-five times. I kept calling out, "Come in," but I'm not sure he heard my voice. He must have assumed I was hurt or dead because he found the RA for the dorm. Since he had recently been an RA, too, she let him in.

I'm embarrassed to imagine the smell of unwashed sheets and vomit. I imagine the room was strewn with my clothes, drenched in sweat from fevers and then left drying on the rug. I imagine the blinds were drawn, if I had remembered to close them, and the phone might have been buzzing off the hook. This occurred enough in the past where landlines still existed with busy signals.

"Frannalah." He called me this because of our ongoing joke that we were actually eighty- year-old Jewish people hanging onto our Yiddish and gefilte fish. At the time, I actually *felt* like an eighty year old— sometimes still do.

"Frannalah!" he said when he saw me. "Are you dead?"

He wanted to make me laugh, but I didn't feel far off from death.

He didn't comment on the smells. Or the darkness on an otherwise perfect sparkling day—all the days in inland Northern California are perfect and sparkling. He didn't say anything about the crusty vomit in the trash can or the sweaty clothes. He probably saw I was undressed because he went to the dresser and pulled out sweat pants and a T-shirt.

"Put this stuff on, lady. I'm taking you to the doctor."

"I can't move."

"Well, that's a problem."

"It is."

He didn't swoop down and carry me like Prince Charming. It's not that kind of story, which is why it is a good story. We weren't close. He had no reason to be looking for me, he had no reason to try so hard to find me, and he really had no reason to spend the whole afternoon helping me.

Somehow I pulled myself up, and got into his rental car. He dropped me off at urgent care. I was mortified and felt so guilty he was missing the game. Through my dizzy fog and screaming joints, I demanded he go back. He wouldn't right away. He made sure I checked in okay, was triaged and put in a bed. Only then did he leave.

The rest of this story is unimpressive. I had tests done, they were negative for everything, and then they were positive for mono. They sent me home. I called my roommate who was back from her trip and happy to help. She checked on me over the next few weeks when I was still unable to move. She brought me soup. She was, and continues to be, enormously kind to me at every opportunity.

That day was a blip in the story of my pain. I may have called Adam to thank him later, but I honestly can't remember. I didn't see him again for years, until at a mutual friend's wedding.

I'm embarrassed to say I don't know if I thanked him then, either. I hope I did. When I think back to the onset of my pain—or one of the onsets—this is one of the moments I settle on. How kind Adam was to check on me, like family might.

I think it's important to also recount a couple of the many acts of kindness offered to me by health-care professionals. I do a decent job of demonizing them here. Many have been less than kind to me, as they have been to the other women I've interviewed. But many have been the opposite and performed acts of kindness every day.

The following are a couple of examples of the many moments of kindness I have been fortunate to receive.

I was in the hospital overnight, and I had a nurse named Cherylanne. She was so small, her scrubs would fall off of her. She hiked them up constantly.

In my experience, night nurses' personalities vary. Either they love the nighttime for its quiet and the eerie, blue light of the machines, or they are doing it because they have to, and slink through the early morning hours hoping few of the patients will wake up.

Cherylanne was the former. I had wounds from surgery, and she was responsible for them.

I am not good with blood, or even thinking about blood or injury, which is difficult when I have my blood drawn frequently. It is embarrassing. Often when I'm tired, or haven't had enough to eat, or feel stressed, I will faint when I start thinking about it too much or when they start to take the blood from my vein. Even writing this makes me woozy. I also sometimes just faint when things get emotionally overwhelming. Doctors have told me this is a vagus nerve reaction, which can get ingrained in my psyche and is a physiological habit difficult to break. I always tell my nurses and doctors this so they won't caught off guard if I fall.

I must have told Cherylanne, or at least one of the nurses from that day, who marked it on my chart, because she knew. She came to take blood around midnight, testing to make sure things were as they should be. I got a little woozy, but was okay, falling back asleep as soon as she left. I dreamt of waves of blood, gallons of it, pouring out of my veins like it was from a broken dike. I woke up sweating and shaking, and had to pee. The dream must have confused the two.

The thing they want you to do in order to be discharged from the hospital is pee. They wait until this happens, because if it doesn't, it could be a sign that something is significantly wrong. Often, especially after surgery, they insert a catheter, but they remove it as soon as they think you should be steady on your feet so you can go to the bathroom. They had removed mine earlier in the evening.

By now, it was in the early morning hours, and I had to go. Cherylanne had told me to ring the nurses' station when it was time, so someone could make sure I was okay to walk. I did, but no one was available, and I didn't think having to pee was worthy of an emergency button.

I sat up. I was clear-headed and stable. I put my feet over the side of the bed, still feeling okay. I grabbed onto my IV pole, using it for balance as I stood up. And that's when things collapsed. I must have taken a few steps because I was far enough away from the bed that I didn't fall back into it. Instead, my ears started to stuff up, my whole body got drenched in sweat, my vision got blurry and I threw up, right before everything went black.

Apparently, I would learn later, Cherylanne happened to pass by my room at that exact second. During the postop recovery night shift, the doors were left open so nurses could peek in without disturbing patients.

Somehow, Cherylanne got to me before I hit the floor, caught me in her bird-like arms, and lifted me over to the bed. She put my feet up, got me a cold towel to put behind my neck, and held a small cup of apple juice with a straw up to my lips. I was disoriented and sweaty, knowing something had happened but not yet remembering what. I found myself crying.

Nurses don't usually hug you. I imagine it is in the training, plus your body is often better off not being touched, especially when you are in pain. However, nurses are the type of people who, even on their worst days, tend to be kinder than most of us on our best days.

Cherylanne scooted onto the bed, her tiny frame taking up only a sliver. And then she started singing. "Blackbird." She lay back to meet me on the reclined mattress and gave me a one-armed, very gentle hug, and rocked me back and forth just a little bit, like I was a baby.

I know this sounds over the top, maybe even a little inappropriate.

But it was exactly what I needed. I calmed down enough to sip the juice. I stopped sweating, could see straight, and could hear again.

And then—this might be the most beautiful of all of these beautiful minutes—she got up, put a hand on my cheek, smiled, and left the room, turning off the lights as she went.

She didn't say anything. I was too rattled to even thank her, and we had sat together for at least ten minutes.

Cherylanne let me experience the moment, as disgusting as it felt, all the way to its conclusion. When I didn't say anything she didn't say anything, but her actions made me feel like I didn't have to apologize or spew gratitude, but could just be quiet and get through it, feeling taken care of. To be taken care of when weak and in pain may be the most important salve. I often feel more secure in a hospital bed than I do at home in my own because I know I'm being checked on. When I give myself over to them it can go one of two ways, and on this night, it went in the way of kindness.

Cherylanne didn't have to help me with such gentle care. She could have scooped me up, dumped me back in the bed, handed me a cool cloth, and berated me for trying to use the bathroom when I was still light-headed. But she didn't. She lay next to me, comforted me, and put a hand to my cheek. She also put a bedpan on the side of my bed so that I wouldn't have to get up again during the night.

Another example of a hundred more happened recently and was a one-two kindness punch.

My primary care physician, who I'll call Dr. H, is a wonderful doctor. She doesn't treat most of my issues, but she is always willing to walk me through problems, investigate new pain, and listen to me as I spew guesses about what's happening based on nothing but intuition and too much Googling. She's kind to me in every interaction.

At Dr. H's office, there is a PA named Joy. I always revel in her name because she presents herself with joy . . . full of happiness and zest for life. I have never been to the office and seen her without a smile on her face. She has always been helpful, never harsh, and sweet even in the most complicated messes.

I went to the doctor for a chain of swollen lymph nodes. They were so painful, I couldn't speak. They pulsated. I had a COVID test, since it is the obvious culprit for everything right now, but it was negative. I had numerous blood tests, urine tests, scans, and X-rays over the next couple of days. I went in for a follow-up. I was in less pain, but the chain was still there, and I found myself crying whenever I tried to move my head. I looked rough. Every person who saw me commented on my swollen neck. It had been my birthday, and even though I felt awful, my friends took me to lunch. When I posted a picture of the three of us, I had four comments in two minutes that something seemed wrong.

Joy sat in a little hallway between the waiting room and the exam rooms. She was the gatekeeper. She called a patient's name when the doctor was ready and recorded weight and blood pressure before the patient went to a room.

As soon as she saw me, she ushered me into an exam room, skipping the hallway.

"Not any better?" she asked.

"Not really, no. Look at how swollen."

"Kids scared to look at you?"

I laughed. "No, I don't think so."

"Well, don't worry, you always look lovely," she said.

Maybe that's the wrong thing to say. Maybe some people would find it inappropriate or unhelpful. But to me, after a week in which my entire face changed in a matter of hours, it was comforting. Joy didn't have to say anything. But she knew me since I was there all the time. And I knew her. And though our relationship usually began and ended in the little hallway, I always felt safe when she was around. The moment and her comment buoyed me enough that when we still couldn't figure out why the nodes weren't dissipating, I felt the echo of her kindness settling in the room. It was a very small thing, but it made a very big impact.

Right after Joy left the exam room, Dr. H came in.

"Hi Francesca, nice to see you," she said.

She talked to me for a bit, examined me, spending a lot of dedicated time probing and looking at my neck. Then, she invited me to sit next to her while she recorded her notes.

"I hate to say it, but I think this might be a reaction to the new medicine you're taking," she said.

I had already guessed this. All the tests she had ordered had already come back negative, but I was disappointed because this new medicine, a mood stabilizer, was the first one that had worked well in a very long time.

"It's okay," I said. "I was feeling all right before I started on it. It's not like I was in a dangerous place."

"But you were feeling good on the medication."

"I was."

"You deserve to feel good," she said. "If you were in a place where your brain felt good, you should get back there. You deserve that."

There was something so simple and beautiful about the way she said this.

I deserve to feel good. I deserve to feel better. How revolutionary. And even if I don't feel good, even if I feel terrible, I still *deserve* to feel good. It might feel like a small click of understanding, but it hit me hard. I haven't done anything wrong to be where I am. It is not my fault. Her statement reminded me of this, and I needed the reminder.

The women I spoke with for this book lit up when I asked them to tell me about their experiences with kindness. In almost every case, the women were happy and eager to recount moments and people who have changed their lives simply by being kind.

Samantha shared the following experiences with me:

"Oh, I've run across many kind people. Too many to count. A couple jump to mind.

"The first was a nurse who figured out a way to wash my hair in the hospital after my accident, without my having to ask. She knew it was bothering me to have dirty hair. Her name was Sophia. I'll never forget her.

"The second was a paramedic who held my hand in the helicopter on the way to the hospital. Never got his name, but I do remember his smile, and the way his simple human touch made me feel that everything would be okay."

Even if we cannot think of specific moments when we are treated with kindness and care, it makes a difference.

Candace told me the following:

"I was talking with my therapist recently about memory, especially about why bad memories always seem to burn brighter than good ones. She pointed out we tend to remember things most easily if they stand out somehow—particularly good, particularly bad, or just particularly different from our norm. I suspect my lack of pain-related kindnesses is not because it never happened but because I've been incredibly fortunate and have experienced very little pain-related *unkindness*.

"Unlike people I know, doctors never dismissed me when yet another image, yet another test, showed nothing to explain why my neck hurt. On the contrary, they repeatedly reinforced that the fact that they couldn't see a cause on their tests didn't mean my pain wasn't real. Unlike others I know, my family never told me to "snap out of" my depression or insisted that my migraines were "just a headache." Friends have never held it against me when I canceled our plans, yet again, due to migraines. So that's what I'll say about kindness I guess: Given the unkindness I know people with chronic pain of both the physical and the emotional kind have been subjected to, I feel incredibly fortunate that the kindness shown to me by healthcare professionals, family, and friends—the experience of being believed and supported—has made it possible for me to seek help without fear or shame and to practice self-care without guilt."

Leslie relayed the following:

"My nurse from my immunology team has been my lifesaver.

"For over five years, I had to commute to Boston for my monthly shot. The stress of timing public transportation, dealing with school drop-off for my elementary school child, and the worry of getting there late was causing my blood pressure and anxiety to be high at every appointment.

"One time she said to me, 'Book whatever time and when you get here, I will give you the shot. No worries if you're late or not.'

"Her recognizing how stressful it was for me took all the pressure off and moving forward my trip to Boston every month was so much more relaxing and the most peaceful time of my week. That little gesture made a big difference."

Michelle shared the following experience of kindness:

"The first time I felt genuine kindness was from my chiropractor. When I went to see him eighteen years ago, he took the time to listen to my concerns. He didn't dismiss my claims that I was living in pain every day, and he was the first to not suggest pain medication or physical therapy. Kindness to me is listening and working with me to make sure I am getting relief from my chronic pain."

Kate remembered the following:

"The kindnesses I remember most were the tiny ones. Coworkers who would notice me having a nerve attack while they talked to me and gently ask if I needed a minute. Coworkers who noticed it was a windy and rainy day and would ask if they could grab me lunch so I didn't have to go outside.

"I had a friend who would wait to leave work so he could walk in front of me and be my human shield from the wind as we walked across the bridge.

"When I had neurosurgery, I had a friend fill my

freezer with soup, and meet a plumber at my house to fix a leaky pipe.

"There was a nurse who met my mother on the side of a highway to give us a prescription.

"These kindnesses were so simple and easy but literally saved my life."

Katie described the following,

"Without question, nurses have been the kindest people to me in my darkest medical moments. It's not just that nurses will sweep in to help me when I tried and failed to make it from the hospital bed to the bathroom and pissed all over the floor, but they're also there to hold on to when the pain was so bad I thought I might die.

"I remember I was supposed to get out of the hospital after six days and because of complications, it dragged on. One of my favorite nurses had said goodbye to me, thinking I was going to get out before her next shift.

"When I hadn't, she ran into my room at the start of her shift, eyes brimming with tears, and said 'I'm so sorry you're still here but I love that I get to see you again' before (gently) wrapping her arms around my neck.

"That's what nurses do. They provide the emotional support that's otherwise lacking in a medical situation, especially a hospital."

Studies show that delivering health care with kindness leads to faster healing, reduced pain, increased immune function, lowered blood pressure, and decreased anxiety.

According to *Dignity Health*, "Recent studies validate that when physicians listen and patients feel heard, patients experience relief from lower back pain and feel better about their care. In a randomized controlled trial of patients with irritable bowel syndrome, patients who were treated by practitioners who were warm, listened actively, and expressed compassion for their condition experienced less pain, less severe symptoms and greater health improvement than other patients in the study. Similar results of feeling heard and supported have been found to relieve pain for patients with headaches and a variety of other painful conditions, leading to a general conclusion that better communication and listening have a positive influence on controlling pain."[1]

Is this all a placebo effect? Do we trick ourselves into feeling better if someone is nice to us? In his 2017 piece, *How Kindness Can Heal*, Dr. David R. Hamilton explains why it isn't. "So, given that oxytocin is such a potent cardioprotective hormone and that we produce it when we're being genuinely kind, we can therefore say that kindness is cardioprotective—that kindness reduces blood pressure, acts as an antioxidant and an anti-inflammatory. Indeed, we've probably all felt that relaxing, calming sense that kindness brings, whether we're the person being kind, the recipient of it, or even a witness to it, and even sometimes a warm feeling in the chest, which is caused by an oxytocin-stimulated increase in blood flow to the heart. And there's more. Oxytocin—our molecule of kindness also helps speed up wound healing. Under conditions when oxytocin levels are low, certain wounds can take longer to heal. Part of the reason for this is that oxytocin promotes angiogenesis—regrowth of blood vessels—which is vital to wound healing. When we get plenty of oxytocin in our bodies, wound healing is more at an optimum. Kindness really does heal."[2]

Love is big. Like I said, I'm lucky to have so much of it. But kindness is often small. Reaching out instead of recoiling. Checking up instead of writing off, texting, nodding, smiling, giving a one-armed hug. A calming song, a cool cloth. A sweet phrase. A compliment. Small gestures that in retrospect, make huge differences.

To the woman in the black T-shirt, maybe I'm a funny anecdote or maybe I didn't register much at all. I doubt Adam would remember this twenty-five-year-old story, or if he did, he probably thinks of it as a couple of hours of extending his RA duties from the year before. I'm sure Cherylanne sang "Blackbird" to lots of patients. Joy and Dr H say kind things to every patient that comes in, day after day.

But to me, those acts were heroic.

In many ways, I agree with Kate. Those small acts of kindness helped save my life.

ACCEPTANCE

A Soft Place to Land

Throughout the last twenty years, I have learned a lot about love. Also about guilt. And gratitude. I have seen the underbelly of my own twisting mind, and the glowing, beating hearts of my truest friends. I have seen my own expectations of how people will respond to me dissolve in the history of our relationship, experiences, love . . . and spill to the floor like sand. I have seen a body cracked and crushed transform into growing and healing. I have seen how halves become whole when disaster strikes. I have been so tired my eyes sting, my back creaks, and my chest heaves. I have found some peace in the strangest places: the seventh-floor sunset at a Boston hospital when the fall just won't give into winter; the easy laugh of my children; and forgiveness in forgotten places. I look forward not to better, because I don't know if that will ever come. I look forward to enough. Enough is what I'm working toward. This has to be enough.

As women in pain, we often feel like we have only two choices: fight or surrender. After almost twenty-five years of navigating this dichotomy, I have come up with a third answer: acceptance.

Acceptance and surrender are not the same thing. Acceptance contains hope—hope that things will not get worse; and hope that our lives can be lived with humor and happiness, acknowledging some days will be worse than others. It contains hope we can do things that bring us success—in our work, families, and lives; hope we can love and be loved; and hope we can continue to hope.

I asked the women I interviewed about this idea of acceptance and if it seemed like an accurate description of where they were right now. Some of them agreed with me, citing acceptance as the linchpin for continuing to enjoy their lives. Some of them did not like the idea at all and felt like acceptance was nothing more than a fancy word for giving up.

I want to honor both opinions, as well as the more neutral opinions in the middle. Wherever we end up, there we are.

Emily said it to me in an interview and it stuck with me, "We are all just looking for a 'soft place to land.'"

Like I did for their onset stories, I wanted to give each woman space to tell us, one by one, where, at this moment, they have landed.

CANDACE

"Acceptance is a tricky word. As I see it, acceptance at its best suggests saying 'yes' to something. It's a state of willingness—active, maybe even empowered. Acceptance can also mean yielding, which can be good, bad, or ambiguous. It can be active or passive, willing or unwilling. A capitulation. My relationship to my pain has probably been all of those things at one time or another.

"Early on, the pain felt like an adversary, a betrayal on the part of my body, and I did the opposite of accepting it. I ignored it when I could. When intentional disregard was no longer possible, I resisted it or fought it. I powered through it. If I could just power through it, I wouldn't have to feel like I was being overpowered by it.

"Pro tip #1: Moving through the world in a body you feel at war with is exhausting, especially if you're losing more battles than you're winning. Then again, I had a lot more energy for losing battles when I was younger.

"My first attempt at accepting my pain was to see it as a challenge. I tried to solve it like a problem or a logic puzzle, but there wasn't always a solution for pain, logical or otherwise. That's always been hard to accept—surely if I just tried harder, I could figure it out! And if I couldn't figure out how to fix it, wasn't *I* broken? (I never said my relationship to pain was rational. Then again, chronic pain itself is often irrational.)

"Acceptance is also used in a different sense, meaning to endure or tolerate. Over the years, my migraines went from episodic to chronic. For several years, I had migraine symptoms more often than not. I accepted, during that time, if the pain wasn't debilitating, the side effects of the medication were. If I wasn't in pain, I was worried about when I would be next. Pain colored everything, either an angry red or a dull gray, which muted anything that wasn't pain-related.

"But I don't really think of having been worn down to yielding as acceptance. To my mind, at least, that's surrender in the face of coercion.

"Pro tip #2: Experiencing both present and future primarily in terms of either being in, recovering from, or avoiding pain is exhausting. It's also depressing, which is, in turn, exhausting.

"Acceptance is probably a strong word for the tenuous and easily breakable truce my pain and I have reached. It helps that in the last few years, there have been a lot of developments in the understanding and treatment of migraine, and some of these advances have made it possible for me to more effectively manage my pain. Feeling some level of agency has made it at least a little bit easier for me to yield when I need to—to accept that sometimes, I really do need to. I'm not at peace with it, but I no longer feel perpetually besieged by it, either."

EMILY

"I started thinking about acceptance as I neared forty. I realized even with correct diagnoses, medications, and specialists, I would likely experience a certain amount of pain and nervous system dysfunction. It was a hard pill to swallow, but I had been swallowing it for ten years. I was used to disappointment; I was so far from where I'd imagined myself to be at this age. But once I began flirting with the idea of accepting it, a shift occurred. I experienced more joy in life, more presence.

"I still struggle with feeling like I've been left behind, but I also have no choice—I could be pissed about it and fight the feeling, or I could work with it and figure out a new way. It's essentially what I've been doing all along, isn't it? I think the biggest struggle is thinking I 'should' be or do or have *something else*. There is a certain freedom in acceptance."

JESSICA

"These many years have been an up-and-down journey. I've had some periods of acknowledging the pain as part of my life and trying to be proactive in managing it. (The chiropractor/clavicle brace guy, various rounds of physical therapy, massages, Pilates, yoga, acupuncture, muscular activation technique, psychotherapy for anxiety and stress, special support pillows, mattresses, heating pads, desk chairs, and footrests, steroid injections, and pain medications—I shudder to think about all the money I've spent on treatments and accoutrements).

"There have been other times of pushing through, denying it as an issue, acting like I was fine, and not adjusting my life at all. There have been some periods of knowing the pain as part of my life and feeling hopeless, angry, frustrated, overwhelmed, and unmotivated to work on it. A graph of this journey would be far from linear.

"I'm in a place of much greater acceptance than ever before, though it is still a very active process. I can now tell myself and others I have chronic back pain, and my pain is likely to be something I'll always have to work to manage. I sometimes have an easier time excusing myself from activities (like skiing this winter) due to potential increased pain. I've transitioned from resenting my pain and wanting to prove it can't stop me, to integrating my pain into my life and more regularly making better choices for me in the long run.

"I'm not saying I don't feel resentful anymore, but it's less often a driving force. The internal voices that tell me that I'm being a wimp, I'm going to be an invalid, my quality of life is going to be seriously negatively impacted, and I cause my pain due to my anxiety or I don't do enough core workouts or whatever . . . they're still there. I try to notice them, let myself feel the emotions, and bring my thoughts back to a focus on making decisions about my behavior that are healthy for me.

"What I know is that my pain is going to be here with me; it's part of my story whether I want it to be or not. I may as well factor it in and do what I can to remain active, emotionally and physically healthy, and to maintain a high quality of life for a long, long time."

KATE

"I had a very hard time accepting I was going to live the rest of my life with trigeminal. Really accepting it. I cried at night because I wanted to find my Dr. Gregory House but all my doctors were the opposite of him. They didn't know what to do with me, which pissed me off. I stopped fully trusting anything they said and did my own research. I was my only true advocate. And when I read about microvascular decompression, I knew it was my solution; I knew it in my bones.

"My parents kept asking if I really wanted neurosurgery, if that was really the right choice. And it wasn't until I explained it wasn't a choice but a necessity, they understood. I think they finally realized they had a bigger risk of losing me if I didn't have surgery, than if I did. Partially this was due to each and every one of my days was a fight—a fight against TN but also *against* accepting this was my fate. It was only possible by taking one day at a time."

KATIE

"I struggle between accepting stomach pain is a part of my life, but doesn't necessarily mean something is wrong and knowing that pain can be a warning that something *is* wrong and I require immediate medical attention. I feel like I'm constantly trying to navigate the line between overreaction and fatal negligence."

LESLIE

"Chronic pain brings you through all five stages of grief. Some of these stages have taken years to work through, but I finally reached acceptance. I'm not giving up hope, but I am acknowledging this is my new normal. I am going to be limited and will have to adapt to how I feel. Life will pivot, and I am searching for new things that bring joy.

"It's the little changes to make things better: a five-mile walk instead of a long run; short workouts with less intensity; more rest days; and more sleep. Most importantly, it is learning to say no to others and yes to myself. My goals have shifted, and I want to enjoy my life with my husband and teenager no matter how I feel.

"It's all about finding the right balance and shifting my mindset. I am going to keep trying to feel better. Boston is one of the best areas for research studies as well as amazing doctors/nurses, so I expect more options to be available. In the meantime, I'll continue physical therapy, massage, exercise, etc. I'm scheduled for spinal surgery in the fall, knowing it might not resolve the pain but it's the next step. I have to try, just in case. If this is where I am meant to be, then I'm okay with that, too.

"My therapist recently asked me to focus on the things I can control. It took me some time to realize that surrendering isn't giving up, it's freeing me of a burden I've carried for so many years. I'm really looking forward to seeing what the future brings."

MICHELLE

"I accepted my chronic pain years ago and my body and mind have adapted to this everyday norm. I know there are others who are much worse off than I am. I'm grateful I can get out of bed each morning and live my life the way I want to. I try not to let the pain dictate my life, and I keep the mentality of, we all fall down, and we get up. Eventually we are all okay. If I had known about the chronic pain I endure now, would I have not attempted a back tuck that day? I would like to say no, I would never have done that back tuck on the wooden floor.

"However, knowing who I am and how I was at nineteen, I'm sure I would have done it another time and at another place. It could have been in a parking lot, and it could have ended much worse. I accept that what brought me to this place is the result of a life lived the way I wanted . . . which is not a small thing."

SAMANTHA

"My solution has been to take advantage of therapies when I can, but otherwise accept I will live with a slow, dull pain much of the time.

"Now I wouldn't know myself if I didn't have the pain. It's been twenty years for me. After a certain point, when you realize pain can be temporarily mitigated but never expunged, acceptance is the only sane response. Otherwise fighting your pain risks being the obsession, maybe the very definition, of your life.

"On my best days, I try to use the pain to remind myself of others' pain. We all are in some kind of pain; it is part of the human condition. I think about a joke my mom used to say about getting older.

"'It's better than the alternative.'

"Pain, in some form, is my price for experiencing this glorious life."

ADELE

"I'm not sure I'll ever accept this is my lot in life, but I have to believe there is a reason I have this pain while others do not. Maybe it's random, but I can't really get behind that. I accept there are a lot of things I don't understand, and I will never understand. Maybe that's enough."

DOLORES

"I've accepted it. What choice do I have? If you accept, you can move forward. I'm just too tired to fight it anymore. I'm getting to the age where I accept everything as, 'It is what it is.' That's not defeat, by the way. Maybe it's calm or something?"

SHEREE

"I accept a lot about being in pain. I have kids, I have to get up every day, and they have to be my focus. What kind of example would I be showing them if I didn't move

through it all with a game face on? Is that acceptance?
I don't know. It's at least close."

———————————

Acceptance is not an excuse for silence. Just because we accept it, doesn't mean we're *over it*. I think many of the women I spoke to would say that talking about their pain elucidates an acceptance they didn't even know was there.

What acceptance *can* do is give us space to look at our pain from other angles, turn it around like a prism in the sunshine, and watch how the different positions give us different light. Pain will always be hard. Chronic pain will always be unfair. We will have periods of frustration, self-pity, shame, and doubt. We will have reprieve, and we will have regression. We will live in bodies and minds that betray us. We will feel good some days just to feel bad again the next. We will know this is the way our life goes. But we will also know we are not the only ones going through it, and maybe that can be a branch of acceptance we have yet to explore—how it feels to experience it together.

APPENDIX

In total, I interviewed twenty-one women, though not all of them are quoted directly. Of the group of twenty-one, three identify as Asian, four as Black, two of Latin origin, and twelve as white (seven of those identify as Ashkenazi Jewish). The age breakdown is five in their thirties, twelve in their forties, two in their fifties, and two in their sixties. The narratives I obtained were either from one-on-one conversations or from emails, and I did my best to leave the stories in people's own words and voices as much as possible. I did consult with them if any tweaks needed to be made. All errors are my own.

ENDNOTES

PREFACE

1. R. Jason Yong, Peter M. Mullins, and Neil Bhattacharyya, "Prevalence of Chronic Pain Among Adults in the United States," *PAIN* 163, no. 2 (February 2022): 328–32.

SILENCING

1. D. E. Hoffmann and A. J. Tarzian, "The Girl Who Cried Pain: A Bias Against Women in the Treatment of Pain," *Journal of Law, Medicine, and Ethics* 29, no. 1 (Spring 2001): 13–27.

2. Hoffmann and Tarzian, "Girl Who Cried Pain," 13–27.

3. Hoffmann and Tarzian, "Girl Who Cried Pain," 13–27.

4. Elizabeth G. Nabel, "Coronary Heart Disease in Women—An Ounce of Prevention," *New England Journal of Medicine* 343, no. 8 (August 24, 2000): 572–74.

5. Joe Fassler, "How Doctors Take Women's Pain Less Seriously," *Atlantic*, October 15, 2015.

6. Fassler, "Women's Pain."

7. Melinda Wenner Moyer, "Women Are Calling Out 'Medical Gaslighting,'" *New York Times*, March 28, 2022.

8. Hoffmann and Tarzian, "Girl Who Cried Pain," 13–27.

9. Tina K. Sacks, *Invisible Visits: Black Middle-Class Women in the American Healthcare System*, (New York: Oxford University Press, 2019).

10. Harvard T. H. Chan School of Public Health, "Why Black Women Face a High Risk of Pregnancy Complications," *Harvard Gazette*, February 25, 2019, www.hsph.harvard.edu/news/hsph-in-the-news /black-women-pregnancy-complications/.

SHAME

1. Brené Brown, "Shame vs. Guilt," Brené Brown (website), January 15, 2013, https://brenebrown.com/articles/2013/01/15/shame-v-guilt/.
2. Brown, "Shame vs. Guilt."
3. Jill Suttie, "How to Listen to Pain," *Greater Good Magazine*, February 17, 2016, https://greatergood.berkeley.edu/article/item /how_to_listen_to_pain.

PAIN PILLS

1. "Opioid Overdose Crisis," National Institute on Drug Abuse, National Institutes of Health, March 11, 2021, https://nida.nih.gov /drug-topics/opioids/opioid-overdose-crisis.
2. "The Science of Drug Use and Addiction: The Basics," National Institute on Drug Abuse, National Institutes of Health, July 2, 2018, https://archives.drugabuse.gov/publications/media-guide /science-drug-use-addiction-basics.
3. "Opioid Overdose Crisis," National Institute on Drug Abuse.
4. "Opioid Overdose Crisis," National Institute on Drug Abuse.
5. "Opioid Overdose Crisis," National Institute on Drug Abuse.
6. Trish Randall, "Pain Patients Like Me Are Rising Up Against Discrimination and Suffering," Filter, May 13, 2019, https://filtermag 158 NOT WEAKNESS .org/pain-patients-like-me-are-rising-up -against-discrimination -and-suffering/.
7. Randall, "Pain Patients Like Me."
8. Katie MacBride, "Restricting Opioids Doesn't Prevent Addiction. It Just Harms People Who Need Them," Healthline, updated

June 29, 2019, https://www.healthline.com/health/mental-health/dont-restrict-opioids#1.

9. MacBride "Restricting Opioids."

10. Centers for Disease Control and Prevention, "Nonopioid Treatments for Chronic Pain," Centers for Disease Control and Prevention, last reviewed July 5, 2022, https://www.cdc.gov/drug overdose/pdf /nonopioid_treatments-a.pdf.

11. AnGee Baldini, Michael Von Korff, and Elizabeth H. B. Lin, "A Review of Potential Adverse Effects of Long-Term Opioid Therapy: A Practitioner's Guide," Primary Care Companion for CNS Disorders 14, no. 3 (2012), https://www.ncbi.nlm.nih.gov/pmc /articles /PMC3466038/.

MENTAL ILLNESS

1. Jiyao Sheng et al., "The Link between Depression and Chronic Pain: Neural Mechanisms in the Brain," *Neural Plasticity* 2017, (June 19, 2017), www.hindawi.com/journals/np/2017/9724371/.

2. "Depression and Pain: Hurting Bodies and Suffering Minds Often Require the Same Treatment," Harvard Health Publishing, Harvard Medical School, March 21, 2017, https://www.health.harvard.edu/mind -and-mood/depression-and-pain.

3. Deepa Padmanaban, "Where Empathy Lives in the Brain," *New York Magazine*, April 12, 2017.

4. "Researchers Identify Area of the Brain that Processes Empathy," Icahn School of Medicine at Mount Sinai, September 1, 2012, www .mountsinai.org/about/newsroom/2012/researchers-identify-area -of-the-brain-that-processes-empathy.

5. Naomi I. Eisenberger, Matthew D. Lieberman, and Kipling D. Williams, "Does Rejection Hurt? An FMRI Study of Social Exclusion," *Science* 302, no. 5643 (October 10, 2003): 290–92, http:// doi.org/10.1126/science.1089134.

6. Alan Fogel, "Emotional and Physical Pain Activate Similar Brain Regions: Where Does Emotion Hurt in the Body?" *Psychology Today*, April 19, 2012, https://www.psychologytoday.com/us/blog/body-sense/201204/emotional-and-physical-pain-activate-similar-brain-regions.

7. Charles Q. Choi, "Study: People Literally Feel Pain of Others," *Live Science*, June 17, 2007, www.livescience.com/1628-study-people-literally-feel-pain.html.

8. Jamie Ward and Michael J. Banissy, "Explaining Mirror-Touch Synesthesia," *Cognitive Neuroscience 6, nos. 2–3 (2015): 118–33, https://doi.org/10.1080/17588928.2015.1042444.*

9. Ward and Banissy, "Explaining Mirror-Touch Synesthesia," 118–33.

FAT

1. Your Fat Friend [Aubrey Gordon], "Just Say Fat: Please, Let Fat People Describe Our Own Bodies," Medium, July 27, 2020, https://medium.com/human-parts/just-say-fat-c2c28e3bb00. .

2. S. M. Phelan et al., "Impact of Weight Bias and Stigma on Quality of Care and Outcomes for Patients with Obesity," Obesity Reviews 16, no. 4 (April 2015): 319 –26, http://doi.org/10.1111/obr.12266.

3. Fatima Cody Stanford, "Addressing Weight Bias in Medicine," Harvard Health Blog, April 3, 2019, www.health.harvard.edu/blog/addressing-weight-bias-in-medicine-2019040316319.

INTIMACY

1. Lynn Schlesinger, "Chronic Pain, Intimacy, and Sexuality: A Qualitative Study of Women Who Live with Pain," *Journal of Sex Research* 33, no. 3 (May 1996): 249–56, www.tandfonline.com/doi/abs/10.1080/00224499609551841.

2. Kristin Della Volpe, "Improving the Sex Lives of Patients with Chronic Pain," *Practical Pain Management* 15, no. 9 (November 9,

2015), www.practicalpainmanagement.com/treatments/psychological/improving-sex-lives-patients-chronic-pain.

3. Schlesinger, "Chronic Pain," 249–56.

4. Schlesinger, "Chronic Pain," 249–56.

MOTHERHOOD

1. Wendy Umberger et al., "The Shroud: Ways Adolescents Manage Living with Parental Chronic Pain," *Journal of Nursing Scholarship* 45, no. 4 (May 22, 2013): 344–54, https://sigmapubs.onlinelibrary.wiley.com/doi/full/10.1111/jnu.12037.

2. Subhadra Evans, Edward A. Shipton, and Thomas Keenan, "The Relationship between Maternal Chronic Pain and Child Adjustment: The Role of Parenting as a Mediator," *Journal of Pain* 7, no. 4 (April 1, 2006): 236–43, http://doi.org/10.1016/j.jpain.2005.10.010.

3. Rachel Rabkin Peachman, "Parenting Through Chronic Physical Pain," *Atlantic*, January 6, 2014.

4. "Chronic Pain in Parents Appears Associated with Chronic Pain in Adolescents and Young Adults," ScienceDaily, November 19, 2012, www.sciencedaily.com/releases/2012/11/121119163349.htm.

5. Sarah Erdreich, "Parenting with Chronic Pain," *Slate*, January 2, 2015, https://slate.com/human-interest/2015/01/parenting-with-chronic-pain.html.

WELLNESS

1. Daniela Blei, "The False Promises of Wellness Culture," JSTOR Daily, January 4, 2017, https://daily.jstor.org/the-false-promises-of-wellness-culture/.

2. Sadhbh O'Sullivan, "Wellness Culture Won't Save Us. It's Only Making Us More Sick," Refinery29, December 14, 2021, www.refinery29.com/en-gb/wellness-industry-issues-perfectionism.

KINDNESS

1. "The Healing Power of Kindness," Dignity Health, accessed July 17, 2022, https://www.dignityhealth.org/hello-humankindness /power-of-compassion/the-healing-power-of-kindness.

2. David Hamilton, "How Kindness Can Heal the Body," Dr David Hamilton (website), May 11, 2017, https://drdavidhamilton.com /how-kindness-can-heal-the-body/.

ACKNOWLEDGMENTS

Some people call their book (especially their first book) their baby. I see the analogy because the investment, effort, and love put into writing is fervent and dear. But this book is not my baby. This book is my mirror, and it is my offering. If I did it right, it's all grown up. I hope it lives within the greater conversation with the respect I intended.

This book would not have been possible without the guidance and dedication of my agent, Jennifer Unter, my publisher, Brooke Warner, my editorial manager, Shannon Green, my copy editor, Lorraine White, my designer, Tabitha Lahr, and the whole team at SheWrites Press. Lisa Weinman went above and beyond the call of duty as my editor, and I am forever grateful for her reads, her notes, her attention to detail, and her suggestions. This book would be just a mess of words without her. Thank you to Rebecca Platt for being the greatest cheerleader in the world and endeavoring on way more reads of my work than any normal human should endure. And thank you to Jennifer Pastiloff and Angela M. Giles, who took a chance on an essay on pain for *The Manifest-Station* and became dear friends and colleagues.

Of course I have to thank the women I interviewed who are featured in this book: Adele,* Candace, Dolores,* Emily, Jessica, Kate, Katie, Leslie, Michelle, Rachel, Samantha, and Sheree* for offering their vulnerability, their strength, and their stories. I would also like to thank the group of women I interviewed but did not feature. Your stories formed the scaffold to the book, and I am forever grateful.

To Carolyn Chapman, Jessica Bissonnette, Dr. H and Joy, and all of my doctors and nurses . . . thank you for working with me on my ongoing health.

There are a slew of others who have supported me, encouraged me, and believed in this book and in me. Thank you to Adam, Adrian, Andrea, Becca, Beth, Charlie, Christy, Crystal, Danielle, Dina, Ellen, Erika, Heather, Jane, Jeanette, Jeff, Jenna, Jerilee, Jill C., Jill F., John, Joelle, Joyce, Julie, Kasha, Katie, Kim, Kim P., Kimberley, Ksenija, Laurel, Leslie, Lily, Lindsey, Lisa, Meg, Meredith, Molly L., Molly M., Natalia, Nathan, Ned, Rebecca, Ruth, Sonya, Stephany, and Suzie for your unwavering love, sometimes incessant conversation, support, and reads! To the women with the golden pens, you have inspired me and pushed me to make this book as good as it could possibly be. I bow to you and your talent, dedication, and support. To Nancy, without you and your encouragement, I would have never started writing again. I feel so lucky to be in your orbit. To Cheryl, Chloe, Michelle, and Sam—I learn from your teaching and from your work, and I feel so fortunate to have access to both.

To my family . . . my parents who have always supported every crazy idea I've had, and my sister who puts up with my head perpetually in the clouds, I owe everything to you three and love you to the moon; my in-laws; my aunts, uncles, nieces, nephews, and cousins; and my friends: I thank you for making up the web of my life.

To my children, Theo and Brieza . . . thank you for making every day an adventure and gift.

And thank you to Nick, for a million reasons, but mostly for growing up with me, in life and in love. The dream keeps coming back.

ABOUT THE AUTHOR

FRANCESCA GROSSMAN is a writer and writing instructor. Her work has been published in *The New York Times, Brain, Child Magazine, The Manifest-Station, Ed Week, Drunken Boat,* and *Word Riot,* among others. She runs writing retreats and workshops internationally and leads an annual intensive workshop at The Harvard Graduate School of Education. She has a BA and MA from Stanford University and a doctorate from Harvard University in education. Her acclaimed instructional manual, *Writing Workshop; How to Create a Culture of Useful Feedback* is used in universities and workshops all over the world. Francesca lives in Newton, Massachusetts, with her husband and two children.

SELECTED TITLES FROM SHE WRITES PRESS

She Writes Press is an independent publishing company founded to serve women writers everywhere. Visit us at www.shewritespress.com.

A Different Kind of Same: A Memoir by Kelley Clink. $16.95, 978-1-63152-999-3. Several years before Kelley Clink's brother hanged himself, she attempted suicide by overdose. In the aftermath of his death, she traces the evolution of both their illnesses, and wonders: If he couldn't make it, what hope is there for her?

Room 23: Surviving a Brain Hemorrhage by Kavita Basi. $16.95, 978-1-63152-489-9. Kavita Basi had a seemingly perfect world—a nice job, excellent holidays, strong family bonds—until she was diagnosed with subarachnoid hemorrhage, a serious illness with a 50 percent mortality rate, and everything changed.

Blinded by Hope: One Mother's Journey Through Her Son's Bipolar Illness and Addiction by Meg McGuire. $16.95, 978-1-63152-125-6. A fiercely candid memoir about one mother's roller coaster ride through doubt and denial as she attempts to save her son from substance abuse and bipolar illness.

Dancing in the Narrows: A Mother-Daughter Odyssey Through Chronic Illness by Anna Penenberg. $16.95, 978-1-63152-838-5. What happens when something unpredictable changes everything in your life? When her daughter is debilitated by chronic Lyme disease, single mother Penenberg descends into the underworld of Lyme treatment, entering into a desperate, years-long struggle to save her daughter's life.

Saving Bobby: Heroes and Heroin in One Small Community by Renee R. Hodges. $16.95, 978-1-63152-375-5. A raw, honest, deeply moving memoir about the difficulties of managing recovery from opioids—the number one killer of American kids age 18–25—told from the perspective of the addict's aunt, who took him in and dedicated herself to helping her nephew save himself.

Stepping Stones: A Memoir of Addiction, Loss, and Transformation by Marilea C. Rabasa. $16.95, 978-1-63152-898-9. Marilea Rabasa grew up in a family riddled with closely guarded secrets, stigma and shame perpetuating the silence. She became part of this ongoing tragedy—until she wrestled with the demons that had long plagued her, and won.